D0891779

Aging with Style and Savvy

Denise Perry Donavin

American Library Association

Chicago and London · 1990

Cover designed by Ralph Creasman
Text designed by Peter Broeksmit
Text composed by ALA Books on a BestInfo Wave4 prepress system
    and output on a Linotronic L-300 in Schoolbook and
    Franklin Gothic by AnzoGraphics
Printed on 50-pound Glatfelter B-31, a pH-neutral stock,
    and bound in 10-point Carolina cover stock by
    Braun-Brumfield, Inc.

The paper used in this publication meets the minimum requirements of American National Standard for Information Sciences—Permanence of Paper for Printed Library Materials, ANSI Z39.48-1984 ∞.

Library of Congress Cataloging-in-Publication Data

Donavin, Denise Perry.
    Aging with style and savvy : books and films on challenges facing adults of all ages / by Denise Perry Donavin.
        p.   cm.
    Includes bibliographical references.
    ISBN 0-8389-0526-9 (alk. paper)
    1. Old age—United States—Bibliography.   2. Aged—United States—Bibliography.   I. Title.
    Z7164.O4D66 1990
    [HQ1064.U5]
    016.30526'0973—dc20

89-28365
CIP

Printed in the United States of America.

94 93 92 91 90   5 4 3 2 1

For My Mother and Father

I wish to thank my *Booklist* colleagues for their ideas and encouragement throughout this project.

D.P.D.

Contents

Introduction

Aging is a factor in everyone's life from the moment they reach adulthood. It is not a condition exclusive to those over sixty-five (as people in their twenties like to think); or a condition of those past eighty (as people in their sixties like to think). It is all of these and much more.

Agingis an issue people in their twenties and people in their nineties should read about, discuss, and celebrate. The books and films selected in this reader's advisory focus on how aging physically, emotionally, psychologically, and socially affects people past sixty. Mid-life crises, for the most part, are not an issue here. However, the books speak to adults of all ages because the aging of those near to them is usually a significant factor in their lives. Further, their relations with parents, grandparents, and elderly friends will color their own ability to age gracefully as surely as any retirement planning program. This book is a resource designed to help individuals find information on travel planning, health concerns, financial and legal matters, housing options, and family relations. To celebrate aging and eliminate negative stereotypes, poetry, memoirs, films, plays, and fiction are also included.

People should not flinch at the words "aging," "elderly," and "old," but they do. Words like "the aged" or "the elderly" are used to distance ourselves from this arena; nevertheless, growing older is a fact of life with as many secrets as the ones tittered about in childhood and adolescence. M. F. K. Fisher eloquently makes this point in her book *Sister Age* (reviewed in Chapter 1).

> The Aging Process is a part of most of our lives and it remains one we try to ignore until it seems to pounce on us. We evade all of its signals. We stay blandly unprepared for its obnoxious effects, even though we have coped with the cracked voices and puzzling glands of our emerging natures (in adolescence). . . but few of us acknowledge that the last years of our lives, if we can survive to live them out, are as physically predictable as infancy's or those of our full flowering. This seems impossible but it is true.

Parts of the Aging Process are scary, of course, but the more we know about them, the less they need be. Plainly, I think that this clumsy modern pattern is a wrong one, an ignorant one, and I regret it and wish I could do more to change it. That is why I wish we were more deliberately taught in early years to prepare for this condition. It would leave a lot of us freed to enjoy the obvious rewards of being old. [pp. 236–37]

Most of the books included here have been published since this appeal was printed in 1983. Pursuing the concepts and suggestions provided by the authors cited within this guide can help reweave that pattern.

How to Use This Book

As a selection tool, program aid, or reference book, this guide can assist professional librarians and others involved in working with elderly people and their families. I have avoided the term "gerontological" and books that approach aging from such an angle.

This is a general reader's advisory for librarians and patrons. A perusal of the table of contents will direct the reader to a specific area of interest as well as demonstrate the overall structure of this guide. The nonfiction in Chapters 1 through 10 and the fiction in Chapter 12 cover the most significant concerns of older people and their families or friends. Cross references are given when a book of possible interest is listed elsewhere.

Publishing information is as current as possible. All titles are casebound unless otherwise noted. Paperback editions not currently available may be released soon. The same is true of large print editions. It will be helpful and economical to check for this information in the annual *Books in Print* when considering a purchase. Unfortunately a few very good books are out of print (they are noted with the abbreviation O.P. instead of a price); they may still be on library shelves or available from book jobbers. Addresses are given only for small presses not listed in the *Literary Market Place*.

The nuances of video selection and purchase are discussed in Chapter 11. Films and plays have been combined in this chapter because so many works have appeared in both genres and because of their basic entertainment value. Because this guide is directed to the general user as well as to the library professional, the convenient video format has been a prerequisite for selecting both library and feature films.

The only hope of mankind is love in its various forms and manifestations—the source of them all being love of life, which, as we know, increases and ripens with the years.

ISAAC BASHEVIS SINGER

The old woman I shall become will become quite different from the woman I am now. Another I is beginning and so far I have not had to complain of her.

GEORGE SAND

Chapter 1

General Topics

The authors of the following titles tackle some of the most significant issues in growing older, such as the cost of continuing medical care, the rights of seniors, and the very concept of being old. Also included are some highly practical books that supply a list of resources on a multitude of topics that cannot be categorized in a single chapter. This chapter is a good starting point for the controversies, problems, adventures, and resolutions that are shared by the many authors whose work is reviewed in these pages.

Becker, Gaylene. *Growing Old in Silence*. 1980. Univ. of California Pr., $15.95; paper, $8.95.

Becker has specifically studied how well deaf people adjust to aging. She has interviewed individuals who were born deaf and those who lost their hearing in childhood. The focus is on people who have faced this disability all of their lives, not as a new situation in old age. From her research, Becker concludes that there is a homogeneity and intimacy that the group develops in childhood in response to their isolation from the hearing world. Becker stresses that this unity aids the deaf elderly to better accept aging and its accompanying trials. Several case histories, comments from deaf people, and basic facts enhance this book. Designed originally as an anthropological study, it is consequently filled with terms from the social sciences. Still, the text is straightforward, and older deaf individuals and their families can genuinely benefit from the information and examples supplied here.

Belsky, Janet. *Here Tomorrow: Making the Most of Life after Fifty*. 1988. Johns Hopkins Univ. Pr., $19.95.

Belsky opens her book with the good news that "today 'old age' starts closer to eighty-five than sixty-five." She calls her book "the first one-stop psychologically-oriented synopsis of what gerontologists know." This may be a bit of an overstatement, but the author does a fine job of incorporating current medical and other scientific research on aging into the concerns of daily life. New research on health, social, and family relationships, intelligence, maturity, and a host of other issues is discussed for the general reader; then Belsky buffers this information with suggestions on adapting and improving life in the golden years. In a chapter entitled "The Generations" Belsky discusses methods for helping adult children recognize their parents' rights to independence and to freedom from parenting. She offers clues for sustaining a social life when chronic ailments, such as hearing loss, seem inhibitive. Some new ideas are presented here with loads of encouragement.

Berman, Phillip L., ed. *The Courage to Grow Old.* 1989. Ballantine, paper, $9.95.

 In his introduction Berman apologizes profusely for his audacity, as a thirty-year-old, in compiling this book. In response to Berman's request for essays on growing old, several people contested his premise that aging is an act of courage. However, many others took up the challenge and wrote about the pain, turbulence, and freedom that come with advancing years. His contributors include authors, businessmen, theologians, composers, physicians, researchers, poets, and playwrights. David Diamond, a distinguished composer, says, "Aging is torment in flux. And only death can terminate the agonizing flow of deterioration." Ira Wallach, playwright and satirist, maligns the term "Golden Age" calling it "a Mary Poppins approach to age. . . ." But he states, "Mary Poppins, however, will be delighted to learn that I do not find aging to be painful or distressing. Age brings with it certain advantages." These quotations are meant to represent the variety of opinions stated so forthrightly and lucidly throughout this volume. There are more than opinions. Experience is also shared. Henry J. Heimlich, a medical professor most noted for his rescue technique known as the "Heimlich Maneuver," describes caring for his aging father during the last year of his life. Actress Rosemary Ducamp comments, "I held up my arm one day in the sunlight and was startled to see all the little crinkles in my skin. Who has been pasting crepe paper on my arm?" Humor, insight, and even anger appear in these pages filled with realistic responses to the facts of old age.

Callahan, Daniel. *Setting Limits: Medical Goals in an Aging Society.* 1987. Simon & Schuster, $18.95; paper, $8.95.

Callahan boldly states that medicine "should give up its relentless drive to extend the life of the aged, turning its attention instead to the relief of their suffering and an improvement in their physical and mental quality of life." Questions are raised on "how the transformation of old age became a goal of medicine in recent decades." He explains how the nearly obsessive battle against aging and death waged by society and biomedicine has usurped attention that should be granted to those starting life or in the midst of it. Then decisively, Callahan prescribes what limits must be set and how this can be accomplished. This author does not write callously, but he calls for serious contemplation of the process of aging, of society's perception and treatment of the aged (calling for renewed respect of their wisdom and abilities), and, particularly, of the scope and focus of modern medicine. Callahan's views on the seemingly endless funneling of technology, money, and energy for the extension of life, regardless of the quality of that life, will certainly evoke ire, questions, and serious reconsiderations.

Cooper, Baba, ed. *Over the Hill: Reflections on Ageism between Women.* 1988. Crossing Pr. (P.O. Box 1048, 22-D Roache Rd., Freedom, CA 95019), $19.95; paper, $7.95.

This collection of essays is filled with insights on women's relations—political and sexual—as they age. It is a result of the founding meeting of the International Association of Old Lesbians. The message is a vital, eloquently stated one on how current prejudices about aging affect women. The essayists explain that women, in this patriarchal society, lose even more status as they age and are perceived, even by other women, as less able, less significant, less attractive. There are some vociferous complaints from women who have become grandmothers but resent being seen by their families in a service role at a time in their lives when they finally have the opportunity to pursue personal goals. In her introduction, Cooper states that "people oversixty are perceived as retired, government-subsidized consumers of age-specific products and services. . . . Those who service the elderly are trained not to identify with them but to make decisions for them, to 'expedite' filling their needs. Old people, like most involuntary consumers, are easier to manage if they see themselves as powerless." This book of lesbian experience holds wisdom on ageism and aging for others as well; it should not be ignored by them. The stigma of age needs a consciousness-raising force. Perhaps it will become a rallying cry of the aging baby boomers (so skilled at protests in their youth).

Crichton, Jean. *The Age Care Sourcebook: A Resource Guide for the Aging and Their Families*. 1987. Fireside/Simon & Schuster, paper, $10.95.

Crichton has directed her sourcebook, primarily on health and housing concerns, to the adult offspring of elderly parents. Here is help for individuals struggling to deal with a place to live, mounting medical bills, at-home health services, neighborhood facilities, and funeral arrangements for an aged parent, relative, or friend. Although Crichton addresses the caregiver throughout, much of the information will be helpful to cognizant older readers; however, they may be offended by the author's tone, which implies that the elderly cannot take care of things for themselves. This annotated directory and information source touches upon matters related to Medicare, auxiliary health insurance, retirement housing, nursing homes, wills and living wills, and possible community service programs. Several worksheets (a personal financial statement, a guide to determine whether long-term care is required or an independent lifestyle can be continued, a nursing home evaluation checklist, and so forth) are neatly composed to help analyze the situation. This combination of information and resource directory gives a good overview, helpfully dotted with the telephone numbers of hotlines, addresses of significant agencies, and other sources for immediate action or information. A final chapter, over sixty pages long, offers an extensive state-by-state listing of state and area agencies—an especially helpful resource for those caring offspring who live far from their parents.

Doress, Paula Brown, and Diana Siegal. *Ourselves, Growing Older: Women Aging with Knowledge and Power*. 1987. Simon & Schuster, $24.95; paper, $15.95.

A thoughtful counterpart to the original health guide, *Our Bodies, Ourselves* (Simon & Schuster, 1976), *Ourselves, Growing Older* was created by the Boston Women's Health Book Collective. This organization, along with over 300 authors, contributors, and consultants, has supplied the information, emotion, and experience that Doress and Siegal have compiled in this unique book. The chapters focus on the physical concerns, altered social situations, and other relevant issues that affect the lives of women over forty today. Among the matters cogently covered are beauty and physical aging, menopause, employment and retirement (including sex and age discrimination), memory loss, nutrition, and fitness. Evaluating such a range of topics as they affect middle and old age is a formidable task. The authors offer a practical, staunchly feminist perspective on maintaining good health and enjoying life throughout these years. Certainly more in-depth information on some of these matters will be required; lists of sources, including books, films, and organizations are appended.

Dychtwald, Ken, and Joe Flower. *Age Wave: The Challenges and Opportunities of an Aging America.* 1989. Tarcher; dist. by St. Martin's, paper, $19.95.

    Dychtwald began studying gerontology at age twenty-three when asked to develop a "human-potential program" for senior citizens. Along with his coauthor, Flower, he proclaims that the United States will be overwhelmed by a tidal wave of aging individuals demanding rights, space, tax dollars, and employment. Primarily for the sake of controversy, the authors draw a potentially disastrous scenario of the seniors' demands clashing with the needs of the younger generation for jobs, housing, medical care, and other vital facts of life. Once this reversal of the 1960s rebellious years (or extension of it by now-aging hippies) is drawn at length, Dychtwald and Flower offer solutions to these intergenerational squabbles. One interesting concept they suggest is life-cycling—allowing periods in each lifetime for alternating work, learning, and leisure—that could replace the conventional pattern of learning, work, retirement. The authors do offer a nice summary of innovative life plans, some of which are currently available, while others would require further societal remodeling. Family life is given an equal opportunity for retuning. Even though it is glitzy and overdramatized, this coverage of the aging boom offers many thoughtful, innovative ideas for creative aging.

Fisher, M. F. K. *Sister Age.* 1983. Knopf, $12.95; Random, paper, $7.95.

    Fisher has been writing this book since she was a child, only completing it while in her seventies. In between she became an acclaimed author on gastronomy, a vineyardist, and far more personally acquainted with "Sister Age." The title comes from a painting Fisher found in a Swiss junk shop in 1936 and has carried ever since as the emblem of her lifetime study. Her youthful interest was piqued by her grandmother. This sternly religious woman ruled the household and her influence is still felt with affection by her now elderly granddaughter. The fifteen stories and character studies that make up this collection have been accumulated throughout Fisher's life. In this blend of fact and fiction, some of the stories are mystical; others amusing; and still others conventionally climactic. Despite the title, this is not solely a view of women approaching or immersed in aging. Fisher is no more sexist than the experience itself. Her beautiful summary of how the aging process is a fearsomely avoided issue can be found in the introduction to this book. She concludes, "Plainly, I think that this clumsy modern pattern is a wrong one, an ignorant one, and I regret it and wish I could do more to change it." She has made a striking contribution with these illuminating tales.

Le Shan, Eda. *Oh, To Be 50 Again! On Being Too Old for a Mid-life Crisis.* 1986. Time-Life Books, $16.95; Pocket, paper, $4.95.

Le Shan is the sensitive, witty author of the "Talking It Over" column in *Woman's Day Magazine*. She is a counselor who has written more than twenty books for children and adults, among them, *Grandparents: A Special Kind of Love.* The same title appears as a chapter heading in this book, where she warns that grandparenting is not the time to "make up for what you see are your failings or your child's—just enjoy." Such stern admonitions dot the book, but they are lightened by Le Shan's humor and well-timed quotations. The words of authors as diverse as May Sarton and Robert Browning add depth. Le Shan brings insight from her own life. Her ninety-year-old father quoted from one of her own books during a discussion one day. Although Le Shan felt her intervention was necessary, her father felt quite capable of making his own decisions and said, "Too much loving protection can be deadly." It is interesting to realize that a smothering affection can rob older people of life. This is not a book full of how-to's; instead it is filled with advice on how older people can enhance their lives and improve intergenerational communication. In this era when "our children are senior citizens," Le Shan offers cues and comfort for each generation.

Linkletter, Art. *Old Age Is Not for Sissies.* 1988. Viking, $17.95; Penguin, paper, $4.50.

Linkletter is probably best remembered for the television programs "People Are Funny" and "House Party." However, his record for community service activities, such as the campaign against drug abuse, has been equally long-running. He has now devised a program for the appreciation and reinvigoration of senior citizens. In his introduction, Linkletter's fond recollections of Walt Disney, Lowell Thomas, President Eisenhower, and many others from his past give way to personal chats with other celebrities, such as

Betty White, George Burns, and Lucille Ball. Their reflections on aging and retirement offer a bolstering prelude to Linkletter's conception of how the aged should be treated and how they should care for themselves. He proclaims seven rules, called the "Golden Rights of Senior Americans." These involve the right to consideration and dignity, proper nutrition, freedom from mental and physical abuse, and freedom of choice in health care, living arrangements, travel and leisure plans, and financial management. Each of these is discussed at length, with suggestions on how older citizens and younger ones can best fulfill these natural, humane goals.

Longman, Phillip. *Born to Pay: The New Politics of Aging in America.* 1987. Houghton, $17.95.

Longman challenges current methods of funding the needs of the elderly (through Medicare, Social Security, and so forth), stating that too great a proportion of the income of the currently employed generation is consumed by systems that will have inadequate funding by the time baby boomers reach retirement age, due to their low fertility and increased life expectancy. He further claims that the baby boomers (working-age generation) face a lifestyle of downward mobility (compared to their youth or their expectations) that, coupled with the rising costs of care for retirees, results in inadequate attention (particularly funding) to the issues of physically and intellectually nourishing an upcoming generation.

This challenging study of intergenerational inequity will undoubtedly rouse many critics; many will quarrel with his figures and predictions. Still, his evaluation of the housing market, including the application of funds raised by federally sponsored credit agencies, government pension and health care programs, the spendthrift nature of modern society, and the simple numbers of the baby boom generation compared to past and forthcoming generations of retirees, provides plenty to ponder. Longman doesn't simply sow seeds of discord or outright panic; he supplies several paths for constructive corrections of this disastrous situation. Longman advocates a national health care program; a method of prepayment of the baby boomer's retirement expenses; an influx of population due to increased fertility or immigration; and a regime of thrift required to rebuild American industry. These options are not simply tossed off carelessly, but are evaluated in careful detail.

Luke, Helen M. *Old Age.* 1987. Parabola Magazine/Books, $7.95.

Luke has undertaken a philosophical journey, culling inspiration from the classics. She strives to demonstrate that aging is neither something to be battled against heartily, nor something one must concede to in misery. According to this Jungian analyst, growing old is indeed a "growing" process. Creatively employing the language and/or ideas of Homer, Shakespeare, Dante, T. S. Eliot and others, Luke considers how to grow old with grace, intelligence, and humor. She has written a new journey for Odysseus in which he travels inland (inward) to uncover the direction for his final days and to impart some of the knowledge his journeys had bequeathed to him. The author does not ignore pain and suffering, which she sees as much a part of this final growing (as an opportunity to "bear a tiny part of the darkness of the world") as is the recognition of wisdom gained. Luke's challenging, contemplative work is not for everyone. Still, she offers a stern reproach to those who long to postpone aging indefinitely.

McKee, Patrick, and Heta Kauppinen. *The Art of Aging: A Celebration of Old Age in Western Art.* 1987. Human Sciences Pr., $24.95.

McKee is an art historian, Kauppinen a gerontologist. Together they have reexamined a stunning array of classic European art in order to fathom its subtle messages on aging. They offer insight into the respect, disdain, or terror with which the elderly were viewed, depending as much upon the artist as the era. In sculpture and paintings old women have been envisioned as dangerous, evil crones, or omniscient, maternal figures. The authors delve into specific issues that reappear frequently: intergenerational communication, segregation of the elderly, reconciliation with death, and mythic visions of aging. It is a splendid way to reconsider both the artwork and the topics. A serious drawback is the presence of only black-and-white photographs; this lowers the book's cost, but diminishes the pleasure of perusing its contents. It is fascinating to see how aging evoked fear in some famous artists and reverence in others.

Smith, Wesley J. *The Senior Citizen's Handbook.* 1989. Price Stern Sloan, paper, $9.95.

Smith describes his book as a "nuts and bolts approach to more comfortable living" that covers the basics on health, housing, income, Medicare, insurance, volunteerism, financial affairs, grief, and widowhood. He defines how these issues are a part of growing older. He mentions favorable aspects of aging and cites the names and addresses of helpful organizations that can fill in the details his brusque coverage necessarily misses. Smith's enthusiastic discussion of the volunteering options available today may draw seniors into such programs as Foster Grandparents or Senior Companions. The latter program pays low-income seniors "to nourish and care for their compatriots who find it difficult to do for themselves." Other concerns, such as travel, are given very brief attention (but Joan Heilman in *Unbelievable Good Deals and Great Adventures*, page 58, has that area well covered). As an overview of the elderly's general concerns and a list of helpful sources, Smith's guide does the job.

Wasserman, Paul, and others, ed. *Encyclopedia of Senior Citizens Information Sources*. 1987. Gale, $140.00.

This 503-page reference book supplies topical access to a range of technical and popular resources on aging. The alphabetically arranged subject headings are quite specific and aided by several cross references (however, the same books and other materials are listed repeatedly under several headings). The material is not annotated, but simply cited and listed under the following categories: Abstract Services and Indexes, Associations and Professional Societies, Bibliographies, Conferences, Directories, General Works, Handbooks, Legal Works, Online Databases, Periodicals, Research Centers, Research Reports, and Statistical Sources. This extensive, costly resource will suit those seeking more specialized material, especially in a variety of formats, including computer databases, professional and scholarly studies, and statistics. However, there are some excellent popular books and organizations listed within the directories of general works and associations. The format may be a bit formidable for the casual seeker of information, periodicals, or books.

Chapter 2

Family Relations

Of all the chapters in this guide, Family Relations best demonstrates the many age levels that these books encompass. The following titles range from books that help parents handle the problems of their adult children to those that address the issue of adult offspring whose elderly parents require their assistance. It is entirely possible that adults in their middle years are confronting both of these situations. However, books are available to help people in each generation. The first section in this chapter describes books on sustaining a marriage and dealing with problems and pleasures brought home by grown children (a woefully overused but essential oxymoron). In the final section there are books to help smooth communications between parents and their adult offspring when aging brings failing health, housing questions, and other mandatory lifestyle changes. In between is a selection of titles for grandparents that offer theories, memories, and practical advice on the task—and pleasure—of viewing life along with one's children's children.

Marriage and Family Life

Gottlieb, Inez Bellow, and others. *What to Do When Your Son or Daughter Divorces.* 1988. Bantam, paper, $7.95.

"You have to juggle between helping out and being used." This attitude summarizes the authors' viewpoint in their primer for parents who must guide their offspring through marital troubles and divorce. The authors delve into the emotional and the practical aspects of witnessing, and perhaps assisting with, the divorce and recovery. Parents have many delicate roles to play—counselor, grandparent (or primary caregiver for grandchildren in some cases), financial supporter, and more. The three authors, who have weathered twelve divorces within their families, offer sensible, down-to-earth advice. They describe the gamut of emotional responses from initial shock through anger, guilt, shame, and powerlessness to resignation and acceptance. Portraying how others have dealt with these feelings is a truly helpful device. The three writers also explain how to be useful. "Home can be a hospice for healing," although limits must also be set and continual nudges made toward maturity and independence. The authors look seriously at coping with an ex-in-law who remains close to the family, and they give advice on friendly and legal means to maintain contact with grandchildren. "Heavy-duty scenarios" (including an offspring's or in-law's problems with drugs, alcohol, gambling addiction, abusive behavior, mental illness, or criminality) are summarily treated in a single chapter. General guidelines, however, recommend several sources for help. Here is sensitive, constructive coverage of a common family crisis.

Green, Ian S. *A Celebration of Marriage: When Faith Serves Love.* 1987. Collier Books, paper, $6.95.

Rabbi Green shares his own lovely, spiritual vision of marriage. He is a widower who has written this marital guide as "a record and a tribute to his beloved wife Frances." They had been married for forty-three years. Green asserts that the personal and physical intimacy of marriage is an affirmation of God's love. His own recollections of his wife and family certainly bolster that belief. Green perceives sex as "set in a spiritual framework, namely marriage." Then he relates how each Sabbath is a genuine reliving of the honeymoon. Moving beyond Jewish traditions and language, he explains how setting a single day of the week aside for spiritual renewal also offers a chance to "recapture the wonder, vision, and avowals" that led to marriage. Certainly his religious faith and intimate affection permeate this book, which should inspire married couples to reassess and rebuild their union.

Gross, Zenith Henkin. *And You Thought It Was All Over! Mothers and Their Adult Children.* 1985. St. Martin's, paper, $4.50.

The idea that the chores of motherhood are endless may distress those who long ago paid their dues pushing swings and playing den mother; but that is exactly what Gross has discovered with her national survey of more than 400 women. She does not exactly see this second-stage motherhood as a chore. Her metaphorical term for it is the "orbital stage," in which the mother—as mission control—launches her offspring into the world but remains their source of emotional, and sometimes financial, security. Admittedly this is a corny image, but it makes the point that a mother remains a necessary, active link. Gross describes the up and down sides of this role as catalyst, arbiter, and nurturer. She cites the ways in which a bond between mother and grown child deepens into friendship. She also discusses the inevitable and endless competition between siblings—sniping among grown children is still a reality, but it takes a different tack from rubber bands and spitballs. Gross is not encouraging an adult's reliance on his or her mother; she simply states that the bonds are not severed at twenty-one, they are transformed. Advice comes from the women interviewed. Their experiences with normal clashes and severe crises can help other mothers (and attentive fathers).

Klingelhofer, Edwin L. *Coping with Your Grown Children*. 1989. Humana Pr. (Crescent Manor, P.O. Box 2148, Clifton, NJ 07015), $17.95.

Klingelhofer "spotlights the almost irresistible tendency for parents to assume blame for the difficulties, the shortcomings, and the failure of their children." Even if blame is not assumed, trouble arises when parents try to direct or pass judgment on their adult children's lives. In his sympathetic, professional guide, the author explains why there are so many intergenerational conflicts in modern society. Incidents of the most common areas of crisis are examined in detail, including "the unemptied nest," a parent's feeling of neglect, grandchildren's visits (that may be used as buffers or barter), homosexuality, or the severe illness or substance abuse of an adult child. These concerns are carefully spelled out through sample situations.

The author, a family counselor, defines methods for seeking a resolution. Most often, he recommends open communication and, when relevant, guides parents and the troubled child to helpful organizations or counseling centers. He demonstrates alternatives to simply paying off uncontrollable debts, taking in an alcoholic, or paying for bail and attorney fees. He also points out when worry is unwarranted. At times, parents must recognize that their own attitudes or methods are simply not suited to their offsprings' lives. There is an entire lesson on developing coping strategies, including a chapter of practice exercises. This is one book that realizes parent-adult child relationships are not a laughing matter. The seriousness and sensibility with which the topic is treated will be a great help. For those who prefer a lighter touch, see Janet Dight's *Do Your Parents Drive You Crazy?* (page 99) or Zenith Gross's *And You Thought It Was All Over!* (page 11).

"It sure is great to have you back for a while at the mother ship."

Okimoto, Jean Davies, and Phyllis Jackson Stegall. *Boomerang Kids: How to Live with Adult Children Who Return Home.* 1987. Little, Brown, $15.95.

The authors, both psychotherapists who specialize in family therapy, have responded to a national trend by creating this advisory for parents and their grown children who find themselves sharing a home and a passel of confrontations. Whether the offspring return from financial, emotional, or psychological causes, the authors suggest practical and sensitive ways to resolve the situations. The diverse reactions of parents and stepparents—guilt, smothering affection, resentment—are explored with suggestions for recognizing and working through these troublesome emotions. Among the practical methods for coping with the crisis is the formation of contracts. These signed records can spell out obligations for all parties and provide an opportunity to air grievances unemotionally. Naturally, the result should be an agreement on payments, duties, duration of stay, babysitting obligations, and similar matters. A reminder to parents on how to treat grown children as adults while preserving their own household is especially helpful. The authors provide comprehensive coverage of a vital area of family life.

Grandparents

Allison, Christine. *I'll Tell You a Story, I'll Sing You a Song: A Parent's Guide to the Fairy Tales, Fables, Songs, and Rhymes of Childhood.* 1987. Delacorte Pr., $15.95.

For grandparents whose memories need a nudge to recall the old favorites, here is a book full of nursery rhymes and lullabies. This volume has lovely illustrations and contains the plots to famous fables and fairy tales as well as the complete verses to prayers, rhymes, and lullabies. Since the classic fairy tales are condensed here, grandparents may prefer volumes with the original stories and illustrations, but this is a good starting point. Allison shares hints on dramatic storytelling and lively musical sessions designed to captivate a special audience of very young children. A convenient bedtime (or anytime) story-telling volume.

Chapman, Frances Clausen. *Grandmother's House.* 1987. Algonquin, $17.95.

Chapman, now a grandmother herself, reminisces about her childhood visits to her grandparents' home in Kansas. Her parents moved away from their hometown before she was two years old, but frequent visits maintained family ties and mysteries. The author shares her memories and dredged-up family tales about her great-grandparents, grandparents, uncles, aunts, and cousins from her mother's side of the family. Chapman calls up wonderful scenarios of holidays and precious moments with her grandfather—with all the feeling of a cherished child.

The existence of her "other grandma" (her father's mother) is mentioned in a way that adds a bit of suspense. Chapman waits until nearly the end of her memoir to reveal the anticlimactic results of a solitary, brave visit to the home of her other grandparents located in the same town. With childlike innocence she had hoped to reunite the divided family (splintered by an ultimatum issued by her father's mother that his wife would never be welcome in her house). The author speculates whether this threat was issued out of jealousy over the illustrious background of her mother's family or out of fear of losing their precious only son, a breadwinner. The visit, but not the dream, is fulfilled. This family rift adds depth but does not merit the build-up it receives throughout the story. A family tree would have been very helpful; sorting out maternal and paternal "great" relations is a bit troublesome. This lack is probably due to the fact that Chapman has altered the name of the town and many of the relatives for the sake of privacy. Despite the changes, the poignancy of a young girl's memory is very real.

Cherlin, Andrew J., and Frank F. Furstenberg. *The New American Grandparent: A Place in the Family, a Life Apart.* 1986. Basic Books, paper, $9.95.

The authors have filled their book of sociological research with so many wonderful remarks, recollections, and reflections on being a grandparent today that it readily appeals to all sorts of readers. Throughout their selective national survey on how the role of grandparents has changed in recent years, the authors encountered three styles of grandparenting: involved, remote, and companionate. The last are termed "specialists in recreational caregiving" and are the dominant style—a result of more openly expressive and loving families, less formal intervention by elders, and the increased leisure time of today's grandparents who range from middle-aged to elderly. The remote grandparents may be geographically or emotionally distant, and their responses explain how this distance affects their relationships with their own children and their grandchildren. Involved grandparents may be surrogate parents or those who maintain an active, formative role in their grandchildren's lives. Special attention is paid to the effects of divorce on the role of grandparents. Current and potential grandparents can appreciate or argue with these perceptions of their lives. They may especially enjoy the chapter filled with the recollections of the grandparents who were interviewed about the roles and personalities of their own grandparents.

Dodson, Fitzhugh, with Paula Reuben. *How to Grandparent*. 1981. NAL, paper, $3.95.

"Who needs lessons on being a grandparent? You just do what comes naturally." Dodson bluntly disagrees with such reactions: "In addition to natural instincts and love, I believe grandparents (and parents) need information in two basic areas: child psychology and teaching methods." Dodson's lessons are smoothly delivered. An overview of child development from birth through age twenty-one includes insight into the relations of all three generations by exploring why children respond as they do to their parents, grandparents, and the world outside. Dodson's version of teaching is not flash-cards, but fundamentals. He emphasizes family rituals, self-confidence, safety, or enjoying a book or a ball game. He speaks firmly on discipline, explaining how to speak with (not at) children. Society has changed and so have concepts on child-rearing. Several examples of family discord demonstrate how grandparents may become alienated if they are not attuned to the present and the adult status of their own grown children. Lessons are dispensed to both grandparents and new parents for maintaining harmony and mutual appreciation. There is also an extensive list of suitable toys, books, and records for grandchildren of varying ages. (Two other books on toy and book selection are also discussed in this chapter— *Buy Me! Buy Me!*, and *Choosing Books for Kids*, page 17.)

Kornhaber, Arthur. *Between Parents and Grandparents*. 1986. St. Martin's, $12.95; Berkley, paper, $3.95.

Kornhaber views grandparents as people who can be living ancestors, heroes, mentors, historians, shields, or undemanding nurturers. The choice is theirs. The author is a child psychiatrist who has spent a decade of research on this vital but rarely studied aspect of family life. From the birth of a grandchild, these second-generation parents will experience new levels of intimacy and conflict. A look at the contemporary variations on the nuclear family leads into a discussion on the situations and personalities that can inhibit or prevent grandparents from exercising their choice. The crisis of "parents who stay children and grandparents who remain parents" is only one of these issues. Problems such as step-grandparenting, physical distance, family feuds, divorce, favoritism, illness, and competition among grandparents are rationally considered. Pat solutions are not issued; sensible, sensitive methods of resolution are. Kornhaber takes no sides in evaluating how grandparents and their offspring or in-laws can fall into roles that block genuine communication and ultimately rob a grandchild of care. Finally, what matters most is: "As far as they (children) are concerned, the more adults that love them the better."

Moldeven, Meyer. *Write Stories to Me, Grandpa! Creating and Illustrating Read-Aloud Letter Stories for Your Young Grandchild.* 1987. Moldeven (P.O. Box 71, Del Mar, CA 92014-0071), paper, $11.95.

Moldeven, the seventy-year-old author and publisher of this paperback guide, describes himself on the front cover as "a too-faraway grandpa." This grandfather-turned-author sets a wonderful example and shares many practical lessons on keeping in touch with grandchildren in these times of mobile families. Moldeven explains how his story-telling techniques are demanded long-distance by his grandchildren. He often asks them for a theme or to finish off a tale. They even evolve joint tales, "preceded by grandpa-grandchild negotiations over the telephone concerning plots, backgrounds, and characters." Moldeven emphasizes simplicity and imagination. If a grandparent is much too shy about artistic talents, he suggests clipping pictures from magazines at home. Audio-taping is another suggestion; videotaping may be tried by the more adventurous (although neither is discussed in detail). The many stories of his own that are included are basic but lively tales, filled with personal references and simple line drawings. The guide is printed on tan paper with brown type and filled with wide spaces and sidebars full of inspiring notes. An encouraging, easy-to-use guide for grandparents everywhere, even those fortunate enough to live close by.

Oppenheim, Joanne. *Buy Me! Buy Me!: The Bank Street Guide to Choosing Toys for Children.* 1987. Pantheon, paper, $11.95.
————, Barbara Brenner, and Betty D. Boegehold. *Choosing Books for Kids: Choosing the Right Book for the Right Child at the Right Time.* 1986. Ballantine, paper, $9.95.

For grandparents adrift in the vast ocean of books and toys for children, here are two riveting guides. The Bank Street College of Education is a most reliable source for books on child development, and these are two of their most consumer-oriented books.

The authors discuss ages, interests, and individual maturity levels so that a well-attuned grandparent can select just the right plaything or book. Grandparents who are not closely in touch with their children's families will find this a treasure trove of suggestions. Consulting the book *Buy Me! Buy Me!* far excels asking the clerk at Toys"Я"Us. The book offers ideas for playthings, arranged by ages and stages, appropriate for children from infancy through twelve years. The toys are readily available in stores or catalogs (several suggestions are simply do-it-yourself ideas—such as dress-up clothes or finger paint). Addresses for the catalogs, manufacturers, and distributors are listed. A serious look at the manufacturing of children's toys, especially the television-based market, considers the impact of using valuable play time aping TV ads. The authors consider the effects of bribery (rewarding good, or even expected, behavior with new toys), the safety and longevity of the objects, and their actual playfulness (do they inspire a richer world of imagination?). After this serious lecture, some helpful ways to cope with the "Buy-me!" syndrome are discussed.

The book on books is equally exciting. Care is taken to describe average interests and abilities for each age group. A book list with one-sentence critiques is arranged by age level, then by significant topics. (In the chapter Books for Fives one of the topics is grandparents!) Over 1,500 titles are described—including board books for babies and, for older children, helpful stories on family relations, hospitals, death, and sibling rivalry. There are mysteries, folklore, fantasies, wordless books for all ages, poetry, and much more. A final chapter on sources and resources can help a grandparent anywhere locate a desired title. These two guides are easy to use, well done, and packed with information. Grandparents near and far can benefit from the insights and ideas shared by the Bank Street staff.

Wassermann, Selma. *The Long Distance Grandmother: How to Stay Close to Distant Grandchildren.* 1988. Hartley & Marx, Inc.; dist. by Rodale, paper, $9.95.

The author puts her experience as a grandmother and a professor of education to good use in this lively, instructive book intended for both grandfathers and grandmothers. This is in a sense a correspondence course for grandparents, since Wassermann suggests methods to forge and maintain a bond with grandchildren using telephone calls, letters, tapes, pictures, and stories in a clever fashion. For example, send a note that asks, "Dear Martha, How do you measure a duck?" or create a book shaped like a banana or mail a bit of outdated clothing for a dress-up day. Wassermann's ideas are not necessarily costly, time-consuming, or complicated. They typically call for a response or activity from the child, as opposed to a gift off the store shelf that demands only a "Thank-You-Grandma-Goodbye" message. The lessons on story-writing for or with children start with simple drawings and move up to family chronicles and involved fiction. There are lovely thoughts about the precious role grandparents play in the lives of their grown children as parents, and in the lives of their children's children. Wassermann adds some tactful messages on handicapped grandchildren. Her notes on grandparent visits carry advice for both sides of the family. Any possible note of reproof is eliminated by the personal anecdotes with which Wassermann illustrates her advice.

Assisting Aging Parents

Ball, Jane. *Caring for an Aging Parent; Have I Done All I Can?* 1987. Prometheus Books, $16.95; paper, $9.95.

Jane Ball tells the story of her years of caring for her aging father. Shortly after she and her family implored him to join them and retire in the small town where he had grown up, this once dignified man crumbled under serious health problems. His memory faded along with his vision and self-confidence. Evicted from his first apartment for lack of cleanliness, he was terrified to move—even to a charming flat closer to his daughter's home. Further evidence of his inability to control his daily life was his wandering about town at night carrying large sums of cash, not meeting his bills, and obtaining a gun permit. When she and her brother took over his finances (at his own request), he picketed her house carrying a sign attached to his umbrella that read, "Avis took all my money." Her brother Frank, who lived a long distance away, did not understand or share his sister's burden.

Ball ends her book with a plea that the plight of both the elderly and their caregivers be granted community support. Her epilogue describes the value of a support group she joined shortly after her father's death at age ninety-four. She closes with a chilling warning: "If your children see you becoming exhausted by assuming your parents' care, they may be unwilling to make the same sacrifice for you." Certainly this is not the most upbeat coverage (and things have changed to a degree, with medical and social assistance more widely available). The vivid portrayal of the toll exacted by caring for a disgruntled and ailing parent does supply a realistic accompaniment to the many practical homecare books in this section.

Edinberg, Mark A. *Talking with Your Aging Parents.* 1987. Shambhala, $16.95; Berkley, paper, $3.95.

Edinberg, a clinical psychologist who specializes in gerontology and family counseling, writes on the need for open conversation between the elderly and their grown offspring. Within even the most loving family, politeness, reticence, or misperceptions can block necessary communication. In a troubled family, even more handicaps may block the sorting out of essential day-to-day concerns. Edinberg supplies lessons on how to communicate, then covers the most crucial issues in successive chapters in order to offer more specific advice. There are chapters on housing; nursing homes; family and social relationships; health, terminal illness, long-term care, and death; financial and legal matters; and confusion. (The last covers Alzheimer's disease as well as the many other causes for such symptoms.)

Sample conversations that work (and some that do not) bolster an appreciation of how people talk at each other without listening. He suggests some practical communication strategies that have proven effective during his counseling sessions. One example is "verbal reassurance which means that your words convey that you care about the person with whom you are talking, appreciate his or her feelings, and respect him or her as a human being. . . . Reassurance can be of great help in even the most difficult of circumstances, because it is the fear of abandonment that makes difficult circumstances even more frightening for older persons."

One of the most potent myths Edinberg seeks to destroy is that roles become reversed and adult offspring are now "parenting their parent." He insists that "we can nurture our parents; we can provide assistance at all levels, including the most basic tasks such as feeding and bathing; we must help them cope and adapt to losses. But we are not our parents' parents, nor are they our children."

Halpern, James. *Helping Your Aging Parents.* 1987. McGraw-Hill, $16.95.

Halpern discusses current social trends and population shifts and demonstrates how these matters will personally affect the American family. Noting increasing longevity and decreasing family size, Halpern recognizes how stressful it is to care for elderly relations. He speaks strictly to the adult offspring or caregiver. As the title indicates, his purpose is to supply information and support to the adult who must tend to an elderly relative. He thoroughly covers the basics, then steps beyond the strict 1-2-3s of home-care for the aged or facility selection. Suggestions on assuring the safety of a household, monitoring health care and medicine, selecting a suitable nursing home, and making final arrangements are included. Halpern also delves thoughtfully into an adult offspring's possible confusion and remorse throughout this difficult decision-making and care-giving experience.

Hooyman, Nancy R., and Wendy Lustbader. *Taking Care of Your Aging Family Members: A Practical Guide.* 1988. Free Pr., paper, $9.95. (Originally published as *Taking Care: Supporting Older People and Their Families,* 1986. Free Pr., $24.95.)

The authors cover the how-tos and whys of caregiving. In the introductory chapters, they explain how caring for aging parents and friends can benefit everyone. Demands and stress are not glossed over; serious consideration is given to elder abuse, depression, and other serious reactions to the toll of caring for a dependent individual. Other critical concerns are crises among siblings over parental care and care by spouses, including partners in a gay or lesbian relationship. After the authors have given in-depth attention to the needs of the individuals involved, they turn their attention to practical matters. There are some extremely valuable ideas shared on how to encourage older people to accept their need for assistance or the necessity for alternative living situations (from live-in help to nursing homes). The authors' sensitivity to all points of view—parent, professional, and family caregiver—pervades and enhances this sensible, emotionally enlightening handbook. Resources, including books, support groups, and organizations, are cited throughout.

Jarvik, Lissy, and Gary Small. *Parentcare: A Commonsense Guide to Helping Our Parents Cope with the Problems of Aging.* 1988. Crown, $19.95.

Jarvik and Small are psychologists who have brought their academic expertise in psychology and aging into a general, public format. Their emphasis centers on enhancing, or perhaps straightening out, the relationships between grown children and their parents. At times, the influence of grandchildren is considered. A particularly helpful section demonstrates a trying relationship between a father and his parents, who boldly comment upon and interfere in the lives of their grandchildren. Like Edinberg in *Talking with Your Aging Parent* (page 20), the authors try to demonstrate the most effective ways to communicate and to patch up rifts, when possible. They focus on such basics as money, food, shelter, sex, and health, and speak directly to the grown children in suggesting how to evaluate the patterns of their parents' lives. The authors also explain how retirement may influence an entire family since it alters an individual's public and self-image. Insight on difficult health care decisions is frankly delivered. More than conversational hints are supplied as the authors delve into methods for making lives more comfortable and offer background information on common health and lifecare decisions. This is a very comfortable book to read, by chapter or cover to cover.

Sheehan, Susan. *Kate Quinton's Days.* 1984. Houghton, $15.95; NAL, paper, $3.95.

Sheehan's story concerns an eighty-year-old woman who balked at nursing home placement and won the right to live at home. Using the case of Kate Quinton (a pseudonym for the actual patient), Sheehan explores the social systems available to help the elderly and their families through common medical/financial crises. The account opens as Kate is being admitted to the hospital for intense pain. She lives with her daughter, Claire, who is in her forties and has had severe medical problems. When Kate is cleared for release, it is obvious that her situation is still too severe for Claire to handle alone. Both Kate and her daughter object to nursing homes. Claire's sister, Barbara (who does not actively participate in their mother's care), insists on the necessity of a nursing home as the permanent housing decision. Sheehan examines their family discord, the hospital care, and the bureaucracy which is set in motion.

A social worker suggests that Kate apply for a new program, Temporary Community Placement, designed to help the elderly maintain their independence by providing home health care. Although Kate is not necessarily a difficult patient, "she makes the acquaintance of 15 home volunteers over the next five months." In this way, Sheehan tells of the social system's successes and failures. Along the way, the author also tells more of Kate's story, especially her years as a youthful immigrant from Scotland, household worker, and mother. Finally when Kate, Claire, and a new skilled home assistant mesh, the reader shares their relief and delight as Kate begins to regain strengths she undoubtedly would not have found in a nursing home.

Shelley, Florence D. *When Your Parents Grow Old.* 2nd ed. 1988. Harper & Row, $22.95; paper, $10.95.

Shelley has written a comforting, informational book on aging—not solely for dealing with crises, as when a parent has fallen ill or met some other catastrophe. Although she does cover the various medical problems common to the elderly (supplying descriptions and advice), she mainly focuses upon the normal patterns of aging. There is an emphasis on understanding and foreseeing, when possible, the type of care or assistance a parent will need. She suggests getting acquainted in advance with community facilities and services (her suggestions range from an economical pharmacy to adult daycare). The book is organized around the chronological patterns that caring children will face as their responsibilities increase from subtle assistance to sharing (or taking over) financial decision-making to settling housing or hospitalization questions. Both home-care and nursing homes are given an impartial, thorough evaluation. Shelley has compiled an outstanding directory for further information; under specific headings such as housing, insurance, safety, travel, and vision she cites a variety of resources, including pamphlets, books, and organizations. The Patient's Bill of Rights and addresses of federal and state agencies are also found in the appendix of this useful, supportive guide.

Chapter 3

Health, Fitness, and Sex

This chapter contains books on nutrition and illness in addition to exercise manuals, cookbooks, directories on medication, and informative sources on specific illnesses and health concerns, such as cataracts, sleeplessness, cancer, and heart disease. Alzheimer's disease has been given its own special section and introduction. The general guides in the health section, especially the Columbia University guide (edited by Robert J. Weiss and Genell Subak-Sharpe, page 34) and Isadore Rossman's book *Looking Forward*, page 33, can answer questions on particular health problems and lead readers to further resources. The premise here is not do-it-yourself medical care; however, these authors, many of them doctors, repeatedly state that a physician needs the partnership of a patient to work effectively. An awareness of the side effects of medication, the essentials of a good diet, and the appropriate steps for recovery from an illness or surgical procedure can help ensure a healthy and comfortable longevity.

Fitness

Bell, Lorna, and Eudora Seyfer. *Gentle Yoga: For People with Arthritis, Stroke Damage, Multiple Sclerosis, and in Wheelchairs.* 1987. Celestial Arts (P.O. Box 7327, Berkeley, CA 94707), spiral-bound paper, $7.95; Igram Pr., $6.50.

   Bell developed this yoga course while she was director of the health and fitness program at an Iowa YWCA. The subtitle addresses an audience with specific ailments, but the author stresses that the guide can aid anyone in need of gentle exercise. Bell explains that yoga in this context has no religious connotations, as it focuses on fitness, not mysticism. This program "combines poses and postures with deep breathing, relaxation, a healthful diet, and proper thinking." (The last is a reference to healthy attitudes on

"As for me, I'm in various stages of deterioration."

eating and exercise.) Even if a reader ignores the common-sense nutritional and relaxation advice, the stretching and more exertive movements can prove invaluable. Each routine is carefully explained and accompanied by photographs (from her classes) and precise sketches. The yoga postures that can provide relief to common aches and pains (eyestrain, stiff neck, and so on) are summarized in a handy appendix. Yoga is a proven method of increasing flexibility and decreasing tension, two of life's necessities at any age.

LaLanne, Elaine, with Richard Benyo. *Dynastride! Elaine LaLanne's Complete Walking Program for Fitness after 50.* 1988. Stephen Greene Pr., paper, $9.95.

The wife of longtime exercise guru Jack LaLanne teaches the virtues and the how-to's of walking for fitness. A good brisk walk is uplifting, burns calories, improves muscles, raises cardiovascular efficiency, lowers blood pressure, and reduces stress. The author, in her sixties, developed a program of dynamic walking that she calls "Dynastriding" because 'instead of taking regular (easy) strides, the length of each stride is lengthened so it is not only taxing the leg, hip, and back muscles, but also the ligaments, tendons, and joints. . . . For any exercise to be beneficial, it has to become progressively more vigorous. . . . The muscles respond only if they are challenged." LaLanne outlines specific routines for walkers at any level of physical fitness. Warnings are delivered for "safe and sane walking" and on proper attire (just comfortable clothing and good-fitting shoes). LaLanne is convincing that walking can provide greater flexibility, more youthful motion, and aerobic exercise. Graduates of this book may wish to look for her *Fitness After 50* (Greene, 1986)—a more general exercise, nutrition, and health guide. For those seeking a mellower pace, try *The Magic of Walking* by Aaron Sussman and Ruth Goode (page 64).

Reed, Bill, with Murray Rose. *Water Workout.* 1985. Harmony; dist. by Crown, paper, $9.95.

You do not need to be able to swim in order to enjoy and profit from water exercise. Reed even warns against making "unnecessary splashes because you get more benefit working under the water" (so hairdos and makeup can stay intact through the whole session!). The reason water workouts are so valuable for older individuals is that "the resistance of the water intensifies the workout, but the actions are nearly effortless because there is no gravitational pull." After reassurances and careful explanations, there is a series of 120 exercises illustrated in black-and-white photographs and carefully defined (with suggestions for intensifying them when ready). A chapter on exercising as a couple suggests some arm movements and pulls that may be too difficult for older people. In discussing workouts for arthritics, the author offers a few specific warmup routines (and numerous warnings about talking to a physician before starting an independent program). The index of exercises sorted by parts of the body that benefit most (legs, arms, wrists and hands, and so on) can be especially helpful for anyone with an injury or disability. Water exercise can be refreshing and fun; Reed's emphasis of that "feel good" feeling should appeal to reluctant exercisers and non-swimmers.

In addition to the titles listed here under Fitness, see also *Richard Simmons and the Silver Foxes* (page 119) and Gary Player's *Golf Begins at 50* (page 63).

Sex

Brecher, Edward M., and the Editors of Consumer Reports Books. *Love, Sex, and Aging: A Consumers Union Report*. 1984. Little, Brown, paper, $12.95.

In 1977 when *Consumer Reports* magazine published a request for readers age fifty and over to complete a frank questionnaire on personal relationships, 4,246 men and women responded. The result is this book, which at the time it was published, discussed issues no one had associated with aging. With total candor the editors asked about "love relationships, falling-in-love experiences . . . sex within marriage, but also about nonmarital, extramarital, and postmarital relationships, homosexual as well as heterosexual—including a wide range of behaviors presently or formerly considered taboo." The book goes far beyond a statistical summary of practices (or abstinence) among those over fifty. Varied comments from the respondents, thoughtfully interjected, broaden the survey into a helpful, enlightening book. The author and editors seem to have heeded the request of one respondent: "Please, not just a factual report . . . but some definitive shoves in the right direction to make it better, more fulfilling." Matters of loneliness, menopausal concerns, and the physical effects of aging are sensitively incorporated. This frank presentation tears down the image of the aged as nonsexual and demonstrates, in their own words, that there are as many variations in attitudes and practices as within any other age group.

Hammond, Doris B. *My Parents Never Had Sex: Myths and Facts of*

Sexual Aging. 1987. Prometheus Books, $16.95; paper, $9.95.

Hammond, as a psychologist, has extensively surveyed attitudes and practices on sex and aging and lectured accordingly to numerous academic and public groups. Yet only once has she actually spoken to an older audience. Those in charge of senior citizens' programs, nursing homes, and so on, explain that "they" are not interested in "that." Such bias in society is the major myth the author is struggling against—the idea that we cease to be sexual beings as we age. Her stern admonitions on the normalcy of continued sexuality contain a necessary balance. "We must be careful not to impose sex upon those for whom it is not held as a top priority" and thus reverse the problem. Hammond explores the evolution of myths and cultural taboos to help alleviate stressful inhibitions. She frankly discusses questions that patients avoid asking their physicians about physical changes and the effect of sex on particular health problems, such as high blood pressure, arthritis, and heart disease. She insists that adult offspring respect their married or single parents' privacy and sex life, as should the staff and administration of nursing homes. There are frequent references to the facts gleaned by the *Consumer Reports* survey by Edward Brecher (page 27). Hammond's book, although troubled by some clichés and superficial observations, is a vital call for reform of family attitudes and social systems.

Nutrition

Claiborne, Craig, with Pierre Franey. *Craig Claiborne's Gourmet Diet.* 1980. New York Times Books, $16.96; Ballantine, paper, $3.95.

Claiborne, the noted food writer for the *New York Times*, offers very cheering news for people who are issued doctor's orders to reduce salt and fat in their diets. With his good friend, the celebrated French chef Franey, Claiborne devised a recipe collection that meets their high standards while reducing salt, fats, cholesterol, and sugar. Claiborne cites his own dizzying revelation, due to hypertension, to the need for a more "prudent eating and living style." This book is enhanced by the insights of Claiborne's personal experience and the practical recipe research performed by the two epicures. Arranged by categories from soups to desserts, this special volume demonstrates that sodium or sugar restrictions do not prohibit the enjoyment of preparing and dining upon a range of fine foods. Jane Brody, whose *Good Food Book* (Norton, 1985) explained the pluses of pasta (carbohydrates) and the perils of beef, wrote an introduction packed with stern warnings on hazards rampant in the typical American diet. She warns, "the truth is that the good life is killing us in more ways than one." She emphasizes how healthy Claiborne's plan is for everyone—whether or not a person has been frightened by the warning signs of high blood pressure, arteriosclerosis, or hypertension.

Eshleman, Ruthe, and Mary Winston, eds. *The American Heart Association Cookbook.* 4th rev. ed. 1984. McKay, $17.95; Ballantine, paper, $4.95.

Grundy, Scott, and Mary Winston, eds. *The American Heart Association Low-Fat, Low-Cholesterol Cookbook: An Essential Guide for Those Concerned about Their Cholesterol Levels.* 1989. Random, $18.95.

These two books are packed with recipes for tasty, "heart-y" food. Reducing fat, cholesterol, and salt in the diet helps the heart and the whole system. The American Heart Association proves that it can be done without extraordinary measures or loss of flavor. In the original cookbook (listed first) there are recipes for everything from appetizers through desserts, including suggestions for appealing breakfast foods and snacks. Among the other notes are special holiday menus, shopping tips, and dining-out recommendations. Dieters will appreciate the calorie value per serving included with each recipe. An herb chart shows many alternatives to salt. Some unusual presentation and serving techniques are suggested for perking up a meal.

The Low-Fat, Low-Cholesterol Cookbook includes a similar array of recipes. In addition, the latest information about cholesterol is thoroughly explained and two diets definitively laid out: a step-one diet, which allows 300 milligrams of cholesterol per day, and a more stringent step-two diet plan that has a maximum of 200 milligrams of cholesterol. The eating plans and sample menus for each are defined in the appendix (following over 200 pages of intriguing recipes), along with a discussion of medication helpful for those unable to reduce cholesterol through diet alone. These two books offer proof that a healthy diet can be varied and appetizing.

McFarlane, Marilyn. *The Older Americans Cookbook.* 1988. Tudor (3712 Old Battleground Road, Greensboro, NC 27410), $16.95; paper, $8.95.

In this general cookbook, McFarlane stresses simple preparation and supplies both inventive and conventional recipes geared to one or two diners. Although the introduction mentions low salt, the typical dash, pinch, and ½ teaspoon are cited in most recipes; an appendix on low-sodium diets indexes the best recipes for avoiding salt, while another appendix cites low-cholesterol dishes. Scattered among the straightforward recipes are tips on setting an enticing table, coping with dentures, storing food, mixing herbs, and safe, sensible shopping. Expanded basic directions would make this book more useful to those (such as widowers) unused to the kitchen; certainly the six-week menu plan is a fine aid to balancing meals and planning shopping. Fortunately, this cookbook is not loaded with recipes so health-filled as to be unappetizing. It nicely blends novel ideas and old favorites.

Wilson, Jane Weston. *Eating Well When You Just Can't Eat the Way You Used To.* 1986. Workman, $19.95; paper, $12.95.

This handsome paperback features pleasant drawings to enhance the 250 recipes, each with numbered instructions following the listed ingredients. Yet Wilson's book is much more than recipes. After establishing her credentials with highly flattering recollections of her New York City catering firm, the author delves into a flurry of advice on adding a special flair to meals whether entertaining, dining as a twosome, or dining alone. Her suggestions are offered in a gentle manner and include many quotations from older people who have changed their eating patterns from medical necessity or to fit a slower-paced life. Wilson offers tips on streamlining shopping, menu planning, and food preparation. One helpful example is the "Cook once, eat twice" lists that suggest how to turn various dinner items (vegetables, pastas, rice, and so on) into cold salads, casseroles, or side dishes. Also included is a variety of ethnic recipes. The diversity and simplicity of many of these recipes make the book a good counterpart to the gourmet dishes found in Craig Claiborne's book (page 28). Wilson takes for granted the need to use less salt, sugar, and fats; rather than dwelling on this issue she offers home economics lessons that promise new fun and healthy profits from time spent in the kitchen.

Health

Holmes, Marjorie. *Marjorie Holmes' Secrets of Health, Energy, and*

Staying Young (Originally published as *God and Vitamins,* 1980). 1987. Doubleday/Galilee Books, paper, $8.95.

"Vitamins, exercise, diet and faith have changed my life," writes Holmes. "They have made me a more healthy, happy, productive and loving human being. They can do the same for anyone." Admittedly this is a premise easily scoffed at, but Holmes writes convincingly. Drawing from her own family crises, the author shares her experience with common ailments and imparts lessons learned about vitamin therapy. She blasts the unbalanced diet of many American families, raising questions about the value of over-processed food eaten in stressful, hurried situations. The FDA's stand on vitamin and mineral supplements is subject to similarly harsh judgments. Following this build-up, Holmes launches into a lengthy, serious evaluation of the need for and sources of (including the sun, vegetables, and health food stores) vitamins, minerals, and other supplements. Her perky guide definitely supplies food for thought, but not necessarily a program to follow without consulting a physician. This advocate of vitamins, exercise, and healthy diet laces the text with her Christian faith. She proclaims, "Although we will all grow older, there's no reason for anybody to grow old."

Noyes, Diane Doan, and Peggy Mellody. *Beauty and Cancer: A Woman's Guide to Looking Great While Experiencing the Side Effects of Cancer Therapy.* 1988. AC Pr. (2554 Lincoln Blvd., Suite 258, Marina Del Ray, CA 90291), paper, $12.95.

These authors have found a way to reduce some of the trauma associated with cancer treatment by customizing natural beauty and wardrobe tips to the specific needs of a woman who has undergone chemotherapy, radiation treatments, and surgery (especially a mastectomy or any level of ostomy). In her preface, Noyes describes her own experiences with cancer and "industrial strength" chemotherapy. Despite routine warnings on the side effects, Noyes was devastated when she suffered "total hair loss—scalp hair, eyebrows, and eyelashes." She sought professional help and found Mellody, an oncology nurse and teacher. Together they developed a genuine beauty plan, from wardrobe to makeup, designed to disguise problems and boost morale. Varieties of wigs are explained in detail, along with correct attachment, care, and styling. The directions on using scarves and headwraps for stylish disguises are handsomely illustrated. The precise makeup instructions include medical warnings along with simple methods for re-creating the look of natural eyelashes and eyebrows. Comfortable clothing designs are illustrated for women who must wear a bag due to an ostomy (surgical removal of parts of the intestine or colon). This matter-of-fact coverage will bring relief to many women and raise spirits and supply resources—a final chapter lists helpful beauty consultants, catalog companies, and health organizations.

Piscatella, Joseph A., and Bernie Piscatella. *Choices for a Healthy Heart*. 1987. Workman, spiral bound, $14.95.

Joseph Piscatella had open-heart bypass surgery at age thirty-two. Perhaps these warnings from a man who has suffered from coronary artery disease will have more effect than advice from doctors and researchers. He emphasizes the lifestyle choices that can and must be made to reach and maintain good health. Stress, inadequate exercise, poor diet, high cholesterol, and smoking are the controllable factors that can lead to heart disease. His analysis of how these health problems have evolved lends strength to his suggestions for their treatment. "Good health is yours for the choosing. It is a choice," he writes. Recipes make up nearly half of the book. The Piscatellas previously wrote the *Don't Eat Your Heart Out Cookbook*. Actually the cooking angle belongs to Bernie Piscatella. She exclaims, "Suddenly being thrust into the world of reduced fat, salt, sugar, and cholesterol was overwhelming." Beyond supplying helpful, healthy recipes, Piscatella instructs cooks on modifying a recipe to meet healthier standards and evaluating the fat content of every meal. For example, she replaces the butter used to sauté mushrooms with chicken stock and the olive oil in a vinaigrette with water. Her cooking instructions can help transform current food preparation habits at one's own pace.

Ray, Tony, and Angela Hynes. *The Silver/Gray Beauty Book*. 1987. Rawson, $21.95.

Ray is the beauty director at a California resort and Hynes is a journalist whose hair has been silver since age twenty-six. Together they have produced a terrific guide on hair styling, makeup, and skin care just for the silvered woman. Their book concludes with twenty dramatic makeovers of women ranging in age from twenty-eight to seventy-two. The before-and-after photographs are not slick manipulations, although the women, with hair in varying shades and degrees of gray, do appear with no makeup in the drab original photographs. The next full-page shot shows the result of careful makeup and hair styling. The authors explain earlier in their text how certain colors and makeup techniques enhance the look of a face enveloped in silver or gray hair. They also talk about clothing colors, skin care (from head to toe), and hair care (especially helpful are notes on how hair changes texture as it grays). The authors relate how to effect "glamour with glasses," describing attractive frames, and how to use makeup correctly with them. Without recommendations, they outline the basics of plastic surgery and a price range for the most common operations (these prices may already be dated). Ray and Hynes have put together an eye-catching, helpful book.

Rossman, Isadore. *Looking Forward: The Complete Guide to Successful Aging.* 1989. Dutton, $19.95.

   Rossman is an M.D. with forty-five years of experience watching and helping his patients as they age. The seventy-six-year-old author states bluntly, "Many diseases are preventable for those who use their heads and make up their minds to act. . . . We are provided by nature with a remarkable second chance to undo some of the damage of the first fifty years of living." He explains just what actions are called for in the battle against physical decline. First, Rossman delineates the basic facts of aging: this is what to expect in terms of the skin, bones, backaches, vision, heart, and brain. In light of these and other predictable, major health challenges, the doctor offers prescriptions (where possible) as common as exercise or as specific as recovery methods for drop attacks (undiagnosable fainting). Within the succinct summaries of major ailments, such as heart disease, arthritis, osteoporosis, strokes, cancer, and hypertension, are "Health Reports" printed in an attention-getting box. Key facts, new studies, and significant warnings fill these boxes. Rossman has an easy writing style, at times stern, but never dictatorial or overly technical. His book skillfully combines the latest medical research with helpful remedies for the most common aches and pains.

Stoppard, Miriam. *The Best Years of Your Life.* 1984. Villard Books, $17.95; Ballantine, paper, $9.95.

   Stoppard extols fifty-plus as the best years of life in her guide to maintaining health, looks, and mental tranquility. As a physician and popular medical writer, Stoppard naturally focuses on such matters as common physical changes, special medical problems, and long-term ailments. Yet her advice on nutrition and exercise leads into suggestions on appropriate hair styles, makeup, and cosmetic surgery. Similarly, her discussion of chronic illnesses and disabilities is followed by an excellent chapter describing various devices and designs that can improve (or make possible) a safe, comfortable home life once such problems occur. Basic issues of aging, such as loneliness, bereavement, retirement, diet, sex, and family life, are covered. The text is enhanced with drawings and photographs featuring older men and women. Stoppard writes in a fairly comfortable, jargon-free style, although her officious use of the word "we"—as in "if we have lost teeth"—may annoy some readers. Many easy-to-use charts point out symptoms, treatments, exercises, and helpful hints.

Weiss, Robert J., and Genell Subak-Sharpe, eds. *The Columbia University School of Public Health Complete Guide to Health and Well-Being after 50.* 1988. New York Times Books, $24.95.

This general guide on aging considers physical, emotional, and mental well-being. However, it excels in discussing the specifics of those illnesses (including cancer, heart disease, arthritis, maturity-onset diabetes, lung diseases, and specific eye, ear, and teeth problems) that often occur as people age. Not a litany of what will go wrong, the book focuses on how to sustain the best health through the last half of life. Basics on nutrition and exercise are followed by good evaluations of the effects of mid-life crises and retirement. Sensible suggestions are made on essential emotional and practical preparations for death. Special charts, recommendations, and other information are set aside for quick referral, while helpful agencies, books, and other resources are suggested throughout this guide.

Illness

AARP Pharmacy Service Prescription Drug Handbook. 1988. An AARP Book published for the American Association of Retired Persons by Scott, Foresman; dist. by Little, Brown, $25.00.

This reference book will help patients better understand the purpose and effects of medication prescribed by their doctors. There are thirteen chapters covering the major health concerns of older individuals, including a section on pain. A short description of the medical problem (such as, hypertension or high blood pressure, emphysema, depression, psoriasis) precedes the detailed report on commonly prescribed drugs. Each medication is examined for its available dosage forms and strengths, undesirable side effects, necessary lifestyle restrictions, warnings on the results of suddenly stopping intake, and interactions with other drugs and foods. Special considerations for those over sixty-five are noted, along with a list of side effects that show how urgent it is to call a physician for reporting symptoms. Helpful hints are offered on handling various forms of medicine, from taking them to storing them. The bathroom cabinet, the most common storage spot, is in a room often too hot and steamy for medications that should typically be kept in a cool, dark place. The clearly printed, nicely segmented text enhances the book's usefulness. Particularly useful are the three indexes: a color identification chart (with actual-size color photos of pills and capsules), a medical-condition index, and a drug index.

Graedon, Joe, and Teresa Graedon. *50+: The Graedons' People's Pharmacy for Older Adults.* 1988. Bantam, $24.95; Jove, paper, $5.95.

Individuals must be aware of the effects of the medications that are prescribed for them. This useful, readable book does not simply list unpronounceable pharmaceutical names. Arranged topically, it contains chapters on costs, generics, and how to take different medications. The Graedons explain in depth how many of the most commonly prescribed medicines can affect the system and interact with other drugs. They have also done considerable research to discover which drugs mix well with foods and which don't. This information appears on handy charts along with suggestions for timing pill-taking correctly. A discussion of the cost of medicine covers pros and cons on generics and includes a price guide developed by AARP. Hearty jokes and advocacy highlight this invaluable guide: the Graedons insist that "good patient points (that is, being a meek and silent patient) . . . won't make your life better." "Don't suffer in silence," they write. "Drug-induced depression, disorientation, dizziness, forgetfulness, and fatigue are often mistaken for inevitable signs of aging." Yet they may be signs of a reaction to medication. Non-prescription drugs are given due attention since vitamins, skin care products, calcium supplements, and so on also have unique effects on each individual. Numerous examples are drawn from the authors' own lives, their friends' experiences, and the letters and questions they have received for their syndicated newspaper column ("The People's Pharmacy") and radio show.

Hartmann, Ernest. *The Sleep Book.* 1987. An AARP Book published for the American Association of Retired Persons by Scott, Foresman; dist. by Little, Brown, paper, $10.95.

Hartmann is an M.D. who specializes in sleep disorders. His straightforward explanation of sleep, its purposes, and its patterns offers background for the descriptions of how and why such needs and structures change with age. These descriptions will allow older people to differentiate between common troubles and hazardous disorders. Hartmann also delves into the possible medical and psychological causes for both insomnia and excessive sleepiness. His calm, reasoned explanations are reassuring. Equally valuable is his simple chart that matches pairs of symptoms with possible problems and suggestions for help (the latter range from regularizing schedules to seeing a professional). The in-depth coverage of available treatments for serious sleep problems will further reassure those in need and perhaps convince them to seek medical attention. An appendix provides a national directory of sleep disorder clinics and specialists.

Himber, Charlotte. *How to Survive Hearing Loss.* 1989. Gallaudet Univ. Pr., $15.95.

Himber's gradual acceptance of her hearing loss and adjustment to a hearing aid are the basis for this fine guidebook to the world of otologists, audiologists, hearing aids, and, particularly, social bigotry. So many people deny their hearing loss because others stop speaking to them and start shouting, shrugging, and belittling their mental faculties. Himber's personal experience will help families comprehend the effects of hearing loss, seek appropriate medical help, and cope with necessary lifestyle changes. Best of all, as Himber relives her adjustment to using a hearing aid, she chronicles the moments of frustration, embarrassment, and distress that many people are too timid to elucidate. Himber was able to cope by gradually recognizing how many other people share this problem. She recalls an experience at an Elderhostel weekend where the lecturer wore an aid and a conference where a woman clumsily inserted two aids and shyly admitted how new they were. Himber's question-and-answer section will interest both elderly parents and their offspring. Discussions cover how to avoid becoming a hermit and how to adjust to a hearing aid. She offers ten commandments (devised by her patient husband) for those who live with a hard-of-hearing person. Himber says, "Hard-of-hearing people are affected not only physically but emotionally, socially, educationally, and spiritually. Nevertheless, they should not retreat to a separate world." This guide can help hard-of-hearing individuals stay in tune with the rest of the world and assist their friends and relatives in adjusting to the altered rhythms in all of their lives.

Holleb, Arthur I., ed. *The American Cancer Society Book: Prevention,*

Detection, Diagnosis, Treatment, Rehabilitation, and Cure. 1986. Doubleday, paper, $24.95.

The American Cancer Society has worked as a research, support, and information source since its founding in 1913. This comprehensive manual reflects that long-term commitment. Part I consists of articles by specialists outlining the issues set forth in the subtitle. Although written for the public, the book uses a level of technical language that may prove troublesome. Still, careful reading can supply a patient and his or her family with the background to understand diagnosis and programs suggested by a doctor and to look for further treatment when necessary. One vital article clearly outlines the known dietary and lifestyle habits that can lead to certain forms of cancer; methods of prevention are also given. Holleb's introduction explains, "cancer is a family of more than 100 types of disease, all characterized by uncontrolled growth and spread of abnormal cells. . . . It is more common with advancing age." If an early diagnosis is made, successful treatment and cure are likelier today. The fear of cancer may be as deadly as the disease because people refuse to seek early assistance. Part II, the major segment of the book, succinctly describes the forms of cancer, their symptoms, diagnosis, treatments, and complications. A toll-free telephone number and a list of American Cancer Society offices throughout the United States are included, along with an appendix of sources for rehabilitation, home health care, support groups, and even volunteer transportation services. A reliable, thorough guide.

Lesser, Gershon, and Larry Strauss. *When You Have Chest Pains: A Guide to Cardiac and Noncardiac Causes and What You Can Do about Them.* 1988. Contemporary, $18.95.

Lesser and Strauss call their book a survival manual. They describe all kinds of causes for noncardiac and cardiac chest pains to alert the reader that "virtually every chest pain is a potentially serious matter, even if it does not pose any immediate peril." Esophageal disorder, skeletal abnormality, tumor, hypertension, pancreatic or gallbladder disease, chronic fatigue, duodenal ulcer, high blood pressure, muscle disease, and depression all create symptoms of noncardiac chest pain. They require medical care as much as the cardiac causes, such as angina, valve disorders, and heart attacks. In a basic question-and-answer format, the authors explain the nature and severity of each of the cardiac problems. Medical treatments are also delineated. Section Three tells how to "answer the pain with action." Suggestions range from immediate emergency reactions to a heart attack, to basic relaxation strategies and exercise programs. Common questions on cholesterol and blood pressure are answered. The authors hope that by taking all chest pains seriously people will not be embarrassed about going to a doctor or hospital.

Levin, Rhoda F. *Heartmates: A Survival Guide for the Cardiac Spouse.* 1987. Prentice-Hall, $18.95.

Levin speaks from personal experience; her husband suffered two heart attacks and underwent quadruple bypass surgery. Her background as an educator and social worker lends the book an authoritative, yet empathetic, manner. Anxiety is a constant for the cardiac spouse and family member (Levin also addresses the children, in-laws, and parents of a patient). She traces the varying forms this stress will take, from the emergency room through hospitalization, surgery, and recovery. The statement "Nothing will ever be the same again" sounds unbearably harsh; yet Levin is simply preparing readers for the fact that this emergency will have a permanent effect upon their lifestyle, eating habits, family relations, employment, and marriage. This wonderfully frank and helpful guide answers many questions, but, most important, it suggests more issues that must be raised with the medical staff and between a heartmate and his or her stricken spouse.

Peck, William A., and Louis Avioli. *Osteoporosis: The Silent Thief.* 1988. An AARP Book published for the American Association of Retired Persons by Scott, Foresman; dist. by Little, Brown, paper, $9.95.

Osteoporosis—literally "porous bones"—is "the end result of painless gradual losses of bone tissue accompanying aging." The authors are both physicians, experts on osteoporosis. They offer an extensive description of the structure of the skeletal system and the changes it undergoes with aging. This information, though perhaps a trifle too detailed, does provide an excellent background for discussing preventative strategies and treatments for this crippling condition. The reasons older people are liable to break bones (especially wrists, hips, or spinal vertebrae) are spelled out and defensive tactics are supplied. Suggestions are offered on safeguarding a residence with guardrails and secure rugs and on lessening or alleviating dizziness, which may be caused by medication, diet, tight clothing, or excessive temperatures. The authors explain the need for calcium in the diet and describe appropriate meal plans and supplements. The pros and cons of other treatments (including estrogen therapy) are also given due attention. This vital book can lead to the arrest of the "silent thief."

Shulman, Julius. *Cataracts: The Complete Guide—From Diagnosis to Recovery—For Patients and Families.* 1984. Simon & Schuster, $16.95; an AARP Book published for the American Association of Retired Persons by Scott, Foresman; dist. by Little, Brown, paper, $7.95.

Shulman, a professor of ophthalmology and a practicing ophthalmologist, shares his technical knowledge of the formation of cataracts, their causes, and symptoms as well as available treatments. He suggests how to select an ophthalmologist and advises on the exams, treatments, and recovery period. Awareness of the exam, surgery, lens options, and recovery is vital for selecting and working effectively with a capable specialist. This eye surgery is elective; as Shulman points out, "the decision cannot be wholly left in the hands of your doctor. Do you want your cataract frozen, broken up, emulsified or homogenized?" These are some of the decisions a patient must make. According to a 1968 study, over eighty percent of those over sixty-five had some lens changes attributable to age; so a large number of people are involved in such decision-making. Shulman's down-to-earth descriptions of the facts and the options should be a great help to patients and their families.

Siegel, Mary-Ellen, and Monroe Greenberger. *Dr. Greenberger's What Every Man Should Know about His Prostate.* Rev. ed. 1988. Walker, $18.95.

Siegel was coauthor of the original edition of this volume with her father, Greenberger, a urologist. This new edition adds current information on testing, surgery, and health maintenance techniques to the basics found in the original. The purpose and function of the prostate organ and the essential aspects of a urological exam are explained. Words of reassurance, coupled with the frank explications, are uttered throughout. Patients and physicians agree on one point: "the longer a man lives, the more likely he is to experience prostate trouble." The problem may simply be swelling or a benign infection. However, considering the risk of serious infections and cancer, the message is clear: an exam for men over fifty or those experiencing any warning symptoms (conveniently listed in the appendix) is mandatory. Siegel lists each of the major prostate problems and outlines appropriate medicinal and surgical treatment. Since an informed patient is more comfortable, this book can bring reassurance and knowledge to the fifty percent of the older male population likely to suffer from prostate trouble.

See also *After the Stroke: A Journal* by May Sarton (page 94).

Alzheimer's Disease

Because Alzheimer's disease is a particularly puzzling condition, several books have been included on the topic. Unfortunately, many people will fail to seek a clinical diagnosis for a loved one, having heard that the condition is incurable. These books encourage medical attention. Some are factual, popular accounts that explain current medical and scientific knowledge, such as *Understanding Alzheimer's Disease*, from the Alzheimer's Disease and Related Disorders Association. Others are highly personal accounts, such as Rosalie Honel's story about her family's care of an ailing grandfather. Practical advice for home care is supplied in the books by Carroll and Mace. Oliver and Bock focus on the emotional well-being of the caregiver. Sheridan suggests simple, practical ways to keep the patient lively and contented. These authors' varied approaches should guarantee finding some help for this difficult situation.

Aronson, Miriam K., ed. *Understanding Alzheimer's Disease: What It Is, How to Cope with It, Future Directions*. 1987. Scribner's, $18.95.

This excellent book comes from the Alzheimer's Disease and Related Disorders Association. These essays, collected from professionals and lay people, are a gold mine of information on this complicated topic. Lacking the continuity of some of the other guides, this one compensates with more and varied information aimed at the public, particularly caregivers. It provides intelligent discussions of the diagnosis of the disease, potential treatments, means of helping and living with the patient, nursing home facilities, and an especially useful look at financial and legal issues. An especially helpful aspect of the book is the tips on finding emergency assistance and on aiding adolescents in understanding the ailment. Additional reading and resources are suggested throughout, with telephone numbers included for the advocacy group which created this book.

Carroll, David L. *When Your Loved One Has Alzheimer's Disease*. 1989. Harper & Row, $17.95.

Carroll opens with a powerful example of the onset of Alzheimer's in a sixty-eight-year-old woman and moves on to provide a medical definition of the disease. He explains why a physician must be consulted, since so many other medical problems can cause disorientation and other early symptoms. Carroll speaks directly to the caring family members or friends, telling them how to seek medical treatment, what information to look for, and how to take advantage of the resources that are available. An excellent section on "Alzheimering the Home" discusses how to make it safe and comfortable for the patient while maintaining the comfort and privacy of the other residents. A section on practical day-to-day care includes advice on grooming, entertainment, exercise, and communication. Many of the author's suggestions demonstrate thoughtful ways to deal with potentially embarrassing or volatile situations. A final section strictly on the caregiver recommends ways to deal with other family members and to ease their burden. The options of home nursing staff versus nursing homes are also discussed. Carroll offers much needed information and excellent ways to keep up the spirits of both the Alzheimer's patient and the caregiver. Addresses and phone numbers are given for several helpful hotlines and agencies.

Gruetzner, Howard. *Alzheimer's: A Caregiver's Guide and Sourcebook.* 1988. Wiley, $9.95.

Many myths and confusions surround Alzheimer's, the neurological disease that impairs the functioning of the brain in a progressive deterioration. Gruetzner devotes an entire chapter to combating popular myths. He also defines the disease, its symptoms, and progressive stages in a concise fashion, making clear distinctions between Alzheimer's, depression, and other potentially confusing problems. Boldface summations in the margin of each major passage reinforce and direct attention to his descriptions. An especially helpful chapter explains the disruptive behavior of an Alzheimer's patient (such as repetitive questions or mishandling money); then notes a typical response followed by a more sensitive, interpretive reaction. The author's advice and information designed to aid both patient and caregiver fill the first half of the book. Part II is a detailed technical exploration of current research, known causes, and possible treatments. Gruetzner supplies productive guidelines and supportive facts for the family and friends of Alzheimer's patients.

Honel, Rosalie Walsh. *Journey with Grandpa: Our Family Struggle with Alzheimer's Disease.* 1988. Johns Hopkins Univ. Pr., $16.95.

The author is the daughter-in-law of Frank Honel, a victim of Alzheimer's disease. She tells about his growing confusion and waning independence that led to medical problems. Their bewilderment over his increasingly erratic, often aggressive, behavior was not clarified until three years after it had begun, when research on Alzheimer's disease was reported in a local paper. By then Grandpa was sharing their home, unable to cope on his own. After Honel recognized her father-in-law's symptoms, she sought medical assistance and began reading voraciously on the topic. She found far more help and information available than did Ball, who tells her story in *Caring for an Aging Parent* (page 19). The author was much luckier than many other caregivers, being blessed with a large family that would pitch in to help. She also took advantage of support groups and other sources of information and assistance. Even with this advantage, the emotional and physical toll of Grandpa's care was overwhelming. This book is filled with practical suggestions for meeting the patient's physical needs, enlivening his days, and sustaining the life of the family.

Mace, Nancy L., and Peter V. Rabins. *The 36-Hour Day: A Family Guide to Caring for Persons with Alzheimer's Disease, Related Dementing Illnesses, and Memory Loss in Later Life.* 1981. Johns Hopkins Univ. Pr., $25.00; paper, $7.95.

One of the earliest, this book remains one of the best discussions of the symptoms exhibited by a person with Alzheimer's (and other forms of dementia). Encouragement is offered on finding a correct medical diagnosis. The authors fully describe typical problems caused by the patient that must often be dealt with by a relative or caregiver. Written without condescension, the book can be comfortably perused by a patient still capable of reading. Beyond the reassuring recognition that an individual's problems are not wholly unique, the authors provide suggestions for coping with these crises. The emotional toll such caregiving can exact upon an individual and a family receives in-depth coverage. A first-hand recommendation for this book comes from Rosalie Honel (*Journey with Grandpa*, page 41), who found it to be an extremely useful resource.

Oliver, Rose, and Frances A. Bock. *Coping with Alzheimer's: A Caregiver's Emotional Survival Guide.* 1987. Dodd, Mead, $15.95; paper, $9.95.

This is the book Jane Ball, who wrote *Caring for an Aging Parent* (page 19), could have used. There are now several books that explain the symptoms of Alzheimer's and various means to soothe, help, and physically care for the patient. In this one, the careworn caregiver receives the most attention from Oliver, a psychotherapist, and Bock, a specialist in neuropsychology. These authors spell out the emotional toll exacted by caring for a relative or friend with Alzheimer's disease. By discussing the gamut of emotional reactions—anger, denial, embarrassment, guilt, anxiety, and stress—the authors help the caregiver recognize that these are typical responses. They also, through a conversational mode similar to therapy, offer suggestions on devising the most constructive use of these inevitable emotional reactions to very trying, painful situations. Some very useful scenarios áre detailed, including how to respond to the patient's accusations of theft, settle confusion over identity, and divert attention from a painful memory. This emotional survival guide makes a fitting companion to the highly practical books reviewed in this section.

Sheridan, Carmel. *Failure-Free Activities for the Alzheimer's Patient: A Guidebook for Caregivers.* 1987. Cottage (731 Treat Ave., San Francisco, CA 94110), paper, $9.95.

In her thoughtful introduction, Sheridan explains that some of the misery and stress endured by Alzheimer's disease patients may be alleviated through performing simple, satisfying tasks. These activities are arranged in basic topical chapters: music, exercise, food preparation, crafts, gardening, reminiscence, family games, and solo activities (games, reading, television viewing, and so on). Computer-generated drawings enhance the well-spaced, straightforward directions. An herb garden, a game of lotto, or a memory book can help a patient regain self-esteem and avoid boredom—two factors important for the well-being of Alzheimer's patients. Family members visiting or caring for afflicted loved ones can definitely benefit from these suggestions. Sheridan also mentions books for adults and children on the topic of Alzheimer's and lists sources for several of the recommended games and materials.

See also *Caring for an Aging Parent* by Jane Ball (page 19) and *The Twilight Years* by Sawako Ariyoshi (page 122).

Chapter 4

Grieving, Death, and Final Arrangements

Coping with death and arranging a funeral is a distressing, complicated matter. As difficult as it is to sit down and read a book at such a critical time, it may be crucial and can certainly be helpful. Survivors are faced with a myriad of questions concerning funeral arrangements and immediate financial and legal concerns that must be answered. They can turn to books such as Katie Maxwell's *No Lifetime Guarantee* for an awareness of the essentials and a guide to appropriate steps. Elisabeth Kübler-Ross is a pioneer in the study of dying and grief. Harold Kushner's book offers help because it does not focus exclusively on death, but touches upon how a severe crisis (such as physical impairment or chronic illness) can be coped with emotionally and spiritually. Books specifically for widows and widowers also offer guidance in grief and recovery from loss as they emphasize how to rebuild one's life. Finally, there are two books that focus on the grief a person feels when a pet has died. Particularly for older people who have relied on an animal for companionship and a sense of purpose as caregiver, such an incident can be extremely upsetting.

Grief

Carroll, David. *Living with Dying: A Loving Guide for Family and Close Friends.* 1985. McGraw-Hill, $17.95.

   Carroll writes in a conversational manner, as if answering perceptive questions on serious illness, dying, and death posed by an intelligent friend. Questions set in bold print precede factual, emotional, and technical responses that share the wisdom of patients, family members, medical staff, and bereavement counselors. The viewpoint of the dying person is particularly well-represented (including the attitudes of "the dying child"). Grandparents especially can benefit from Carroll's explication of children's views on death and funerals. The author shares new insights on whether to inform a terminal patient about the severity of the illness. He provides a keen analysis of Kübler-Ross's research. The practical angle is as well-covered as the emotional one, with discussions of home care, hospices, the living will, counseling, funeral and memorial services, and support groups. Carroll's book is certain to open communication among friends and family.

Donnelly, Katherine Fair. *Recovering from the Loss of a Parent: Adult Sons and Daughters Reveal How They Overcame Their Grief.* 1987. Dodd, Mead, $16.95; paper, $8.95.

Donnelly speaks to adults about coping with the death of a parent. Most significantly, she demonstrates how sharing grief is one of the major steps to recovery. Her book is filled with heart-wrenching experiences of bereaved sons and daughters. These stories are thoughtfully used to demonstrate the initial feelings of shock, loss, anger, guilt, and sorrow. Real-life events not only lend emotional impact, but also demonstrate the differing feelings among family members. Not all child-parent relationships are the same nor are they perfect. To help understand this, accounts of animosity among siblings, problems with the surviving parent, and clashes with a less-than-understanding spouse are cited. For people whose grief cannot be outgrown, Donnelly discusses the value of counseling and special support groups and emphasizes the comfort that can be drawn from friends and relatives. Equally valuable are the author's other two books, *Recovering from the Loss of a Child* and *Recovering from the Loss of a Sibling.* The former speaks to parents of younger children, while the latter informs teens and adults on how the trauma of the death of a brother or sister during childhood can continue to affect them as an adult. Donnelly's books can supply guidance for concerned friends and bereaved family members. She suggests a role model for bereavement support programs and a national listing of helpful organizations.

Kübler-Ross, Elisabeth. *On Death and Dying.* 1969. Macmillan, paper, $5.95.

In this landmark study, Kübler-Ross clarifies the five stages of mourning that are part of the terminally ill's emotional journey to death along with the steps a grieving individual takes on the road to recovery. These encompass: shock, denial, anger, bargaining, depression, and acceptance. Naturally no one travels simply from one state of emotion to another. Kübler-Ross draws on her extensive hospital and hospice experience to demonstrate how individuals move from and between these psychological states. The author's perspective is very much with the patient. There have been many more books on grief and illness since this significant resource opened the doors for work with the terminally ill; yet most refer back to this volume.

The realization of such progress, or growth, experienced by a person heading for a cataclysm in life has been transferred by other authors to situations other than death. One author capably used these stages as an explanation of how adults come to accept their own or parents' overall aging and decline. With so much quoting and extension of her original ideas, it is very helpful to return to this initial, triumphant book. In a later volume, *Death, the Final Stages of Growth* (Prentice-Hall, 1975), she wrote, "Learning to invest yourself in living when you have lost someone you love is very difficult, but only through doing so can you give some meaning to that person's death."

See also *To Live until You Die*, a library video on Kübler-Ross (page 120).

Kushner, Harold S. *When Bad Things Happen to Good People.* 1981. Schocken, $13.95; Avon, paper, $3.95.

In the opening pages the author establishes his qualifications for writing this book with an account of his own sorrow. He was a young rabbi when he learned that his "happy, outgoing three-year-old" suffered from progeria (rapid aging) and would certainly die before or during his adolescence. Kushner's experiences do not overwhelm the book, but they do explain how in fifteen years as a parent and a religious counselor he has heard and uttered such questions as: "How could God do this to me?" or "Why do I deserve this pain and suffering?" And he tries to find an answer. By studying the story of Job, he bravely reassesses the concept of God's will: "God does not cause our misfortunes. Some are caused by bad luck, some are caused by bad people, and some are simply an inevitable consequence of our being human and being mortal, living in a world of inflexible natural laws. . . . Because tragedy is not God's will we need not feel hurt or betrayed by God when tragedy strikes." Readers may question the author's philosophy and conclusions (his religion is unobtrusive); yet this book is, after all, a personal attempt to answer an unanswerable question. One of his conclusions is that the title should be altered to "Now that this has happened to me, what am I going to do about it?" Kushner's ideas, delivered with sensitivity and intelligent grace, may offer comfort, support, and food for thought to people stricken by the death of a loved one, a serious illness, or any other calamities that try their faith.

Rollin, Betty. *Last Wish*. 1985. Simon & Schuster, $14.95; Warner, paper, $8.95; G. K. Hall Large Print Books, $15.95.

Rollin originally wrote about cancer in *First, You Cry* (Lippincott, 1976)—the story of her own bout with breast cancer and mastectomy. With equal candor she has written this controversial account of her mother's euthanasia. Rollin describes her mother as a "garden variety short, plump, occasionally over-rouged Jewish lady." After being diagnosed with ovarian cancer, operated upon, and treated with debilitating chemotherapy ("a descent into hell") her mother was "sick, weak, bald, and by now, stripped of illusion. . . ." Ida Rollin died "not when death summoned her, but when she summoned death." She asked her daughter to discover exactly what medication would provide a definitive lethal dose. To do this, Rollin surreptitiously queried friends in the medical profession. She was directed to an American doctor in Amsterdam who suggested exactly what type and quantity of pills Ida could take to end her life. Rollin describes her mother's decision-making: "I don't think for a moment that what I'm going through is any worse than what a lot of people suffer who want to live. What do I need to hang on for? Life has given me seventy-six wonderful years." Rollin and her husband sat with her mother, cheering her on as she took her pills and fulfilled her "last wish." Finally, Rollin quotes the outspoken advocate from Amsterdam: "Modern medicine has done a great job of prolonging life, but the legal system hasn't caught up with the difficulties that inevitably arise when you have people living longer than they want to live."

Wennberg, Robert N. *Terminal Choices: Euthanasia, Suicide, and the Right to Die*. 1989. Eerdmans, paper, $13.95.

Wennberg contemplates "terminal choices—reflecting on how we should die and how we should encourage others to die." The distinctions between refusal of treatment, active euthanasia, treatment withdrawal, and suicide are carefully spelled out by Wennberg, who has called on several legal, medical, and religious authorities to offer their comments on this controversial matter. The author, who is an ordained Presbyterian minister and professor of philosophy, outlines the dissenting moral stances on active and passive euthanasia. He reaches back to the Greek and Roman philosophers in tracing his study of social approbation and disapproval, then applies such historic thinking to the quandaries created by modern medicine. After sorting through the layers of controversy, Wennberg quietly states his own views on the legalization of euthanasia. This is a more profound book than Irving Sloan's survey of legal precedent, *The Right to Die* (page 82).

Widows and Widowers

Ashton, Betsy. *Betsy Ashton's Guide to Living on Your Own.* 1988. Little, Brown, paper, $12.95.

Ashton, a television journalist and specialist in consumer affairs, has drawn upon her experience with the CBS "Morning Program" and other news shows to produce a terrific guide for the neophyte in personal financial matters. Although she seems to be addressing the single young woman who has recently left the security of her home and parental credit card, many older people are equally sheltered from handling financial affairs. So, most of the advice is valid for the older man or woman (especially the newly widowed) who has questions about setting up a household or credit records. Ashton's explanations start with how to open a checking account (without getting caught by fees and massive deposit requirements) and increase in complexity to the rental of an apartment or condo (no other housing options are explored). She also touches upon the basics of utilities, telephone services, shopping (by phone, computer, television, or mail), taxes, and health and life insurance. Her handy introduction to the real world has helpful references to books that can compensate for her superficial coverage. Ashton's style is as informative and breezy as a TV broadcast, with all of the issues thoughtfully listed in the table of contents.

Caine, Lynn. *Being a Widow.* 1988. Arbor, $18.95.

In 1974 Caine published *Widow* about her own experiences. Her husband died suddenly, leaving her with two small children and inadequate financial means. Ironically, it was the story of her grief and recovery that "catapulted her into a fifteen-year odyssey of lectures, seminars, book-promotion tours, and television and radio appearances." This book is not about her career, but about the basics of survival for widows. Caine talks frankly about coping with a spouse's terminal illness and about physically living with the shock of loss and the resulting emotional, practical, and physical problems. She counsels women literally on how to eat, sleep, express grief, and regain contact with the outside world. Steps toward recovery are also offered along with advice on dating, sex, assertive behavior, and creating a new, personal lifestyle. Lists of helpful organizations and suggested books are appended. Caine has supplemented examples from her own experience with quoted letters and comments from the thousands of women who have responded to her writing and talks. In an epilogue she openly discusses being diagnosed and treated for cancer. How she managed to explain this tragedy to her two adult children offers a lesson on candid communication.

Campbell, Scott, with Phyllis R. Silverman. *Widower: When Men Are Left Alone.* 1987. Prentice-Hall, $17.95.

  Consisting of first-person accounts from twenty widowers, this book demonstrates how they coped with their individual losses. Campbell and Silverman realized that men are "more adrift in widowhood than women" because they often lack close friendships with peers and refuse to seek help. These genuine stories of grief, bereavement, and recovery, augmented by the authors' commentaries, should help. The stories are shattering. The wife of one young man, age forty-one, was murdered; he tells how his family has aided his recovery as well as that of his children. Another man, Derek Humphrey, fulfilled his wife's request for a lethal dose of drugs to end her pain from an incurable cancer. This difficult decision, described in Humphrey's book, *Jean's Way*, led him to the formation of a national organization, the Hemlock Society, which champions euthanasia. Campbell's book is difficult to read. Still, the anguish of sharing the pain these men faced can be cathartic. Furthermore, since the widowers bluntly state how expressions of sympathy were often misguided (even well-intended remarks on dating or remarriage), such knowledge can aid family members, friends, and professionals in speaking to and assisting the bereaved.

DiGiulio, Robert C. *Beyond Widowhood: From Bereavement to Emergence and Hope.* 1989. Free Pr., $19.95.

  DiGiulio was widowed when his wife, daughter, and in-laws were killed in a car accident. His experiences pervade this book, but it is also filled with the anguish and reconciliation of many other widowed men and women who shared their feelings with him. A middle-aged man with small children, DiGiulio has sought out people in similar circumstances. He neither excludes elderly people, nor does he write exclusively for the aged, either. It is interesting to see how experiences differ over the years, and how men and women respond differently to loss. His book is not primarily a lesson on enduring grief. He focuses on restructuring a person's identity and life as a result of these new circumstances: "Widows and widowers must face not only personal grief and issues of adaptation to the death of their spouses, but also the sudden devalued status of not being married." He addresses social and financial losses incurred by the widowed person—matters not usually explored in books on grieving with a focus on the return to normal life. A woman whose identity has depended solely on her marriage and motherhood will face a challenge to restructure her sense of self. DiGiulio perceives widowhood as a growth process resulting in a "transformation." Advice is given on securing the assistance of support groups, family members, and friends. By speaking with so many widowed people, DiGiulio found an opportunity to accept and express his own feelings. His book will do that for others.

Graham, Virginia. *Life after Harry: My Adventures in Widowhood.* 1988. Simon & Schuster, $17.95.

Graham was seventy-four and had been a widow for eight years when she wrote this book. She opens by asking, "Is there life after Harry?"—even though her subtitle answers that widowhood is an adventure. Graham offers advice on dating, regaining self-esteem, keeping busy, family life, and decision-making. She shares her experiences in a chatty tone, similar to that of her talk shows, "Girl Talk" (from the 1960s) and "The Virginia Graham Show" (1970–1973). She comments openly about loneliness and feelings of betrayal, powerlessness, and depression—but only briefly. Soon she is regaling her readers with anecdotes about blind dates and video-dating services. Vehemently and repeatedly Graham exclaims, "If I could impart just one piece of wisdom to my fellow widows, it is this: don't be so eager to find company that you should be willing to suffer jerks." She looks at the positive side of living alone and makes suggestions on filling home, schedule, and life with a zestful independence. Graham even tucks in a few favorite recipes in her section on rebuilding a social life. A word of warning: this book definitely speaks to women who are on the recovery side of their grief. Her upsy-daisy demeanor may be hard to take for the newly widowed.

Mall, E. Jane. *And God Created Wrinkles.* 1988. Ballantine/Epiphany, $14.95.

Mall presents her own Christian-oriented outlook on aging. Her experiences as a single mother and, now widowed for twenty years, as a solitary, aging woman highlight this book filled with advice for her peers. Among her recommendations: don't manipulate your children with sob stories about loneliness, feigned illness, or the more attentive children of your friends; don't vegetate in front of the television all day; and don't lecture the young on prurient behavior just because you can't recall your last sexual experience. There are lists of do's as well: unwrap your fine china and silver—you're worth it; keep moving—both brain and body; treasure your independence; keep in touch with children and grandchildren (even if they seem too busy); learn to listen; and prepare—spiritually, emotionally, and practically—for death. Mall's attitude ("we're old, so what") should help as much as her guidance on the particular problems of older, solitary women.

Weaver, Frances. *The Girls with the Grandmother Faces: Single and Sixty Is Not for Sissies.* 1987. Midlife Musings (P.O. Box 129, Lake George, NY 12845), paper, $5.95.

A peppy get-back-into-the-stream-of-things (or reroute the river) book for widows. Weaver was widowed at fifty-five. She sees widowhood as a "rite of passage in the strongest sense of the word. Our lives have changed and can never be the same again. The friends, the social life, the financial priorities, our relationships with our children, daily routines and leisure time, the way we eat and the way we sleep are all new." Weaver tells how to make the best of this situation—not just how to cope. For example, she learned how to fly a kite and joined a kite-flying club that has brought her international adventures and plenty of writing material. She left her Colorado home for a school in the Adirondacks to study writing: this upbeat, ingenuous guide is the result. She covers topics not discussed in Virginia Graham's similar sermon (page 50), such as the changing relationship with one's adult children and the socially stimulating advantages of continuing education. Weaver enthusiastically supports Elderhostel (discussed in Mildred Hyman's *Elderhostels: The Students' Choice*, page 59) and similar programs. This slim paperback is filled with encouragement and resourceful schemes for widows or widowers.

See also Liz Carpenter's *Getting Better All the Time* (page 88).

Funerals and Final Arrangements

Carlson, Lisa. *Caring for Your Own Dead.* 1987. Upper Access (One Upper Access Road, P.O. Box 457, Hinesburg, VT 05461), $17.95; paper, $12.95.

As the title bluntly states, this is a handbook for making final arrangements after the death of a loved one. Unlike the other books reviewed in this section, Carlson provides a state-by-state directory of funeral regulations, policies, resources, and services. Laws on death certificates, body transportation, private burial, and cremation are spelled out; lists of crematories include addresses, phone numbers, requirements, and costs. Similar information is given on donating the body for medical research. Carlson precedes this informative directory with a short history that clarifies the precedents and current practices of public burials, embalming (actually nonessential except to delay the funeral), cremation, and body donation. This straightforward, almost encyclopedic recitation of significant and little-considered information is too dramatically introduced by three scenarios of privately made arrangements. The first is a grim account of suicide with little money left to pay for a conventional funeral home. The other true stories, meant to show the feasibility of planning and executing funerals on one's own, may put some people off since they are very homespun—involving home-built pine caskets and hilltop services; yet the packaged services of a funeral home may not always offer mourners the most appropriate, personal service or one that is financially feasible. So Carlson's book, despite its drawbacks, is important.

Funerals: Consumer's Last Rights. Ed. by the Editors of *Consumer Reports.* 1987. Norton, $10.95.

With their usual vigor and critical acumen, the editors of *Consumers Reports* investigated the funeral industry in the United States. They explain in the introduction, "Our purpose was not to write an exposé of the funeral industry, although we find good reason to be critical of it. . . . This book has two purposes. One is to help readers become better informed about conventional funerals and burial . . . as well as less costly alternatives. The other purpose is to provide practical information about the choices and the decisions that most survivors must face only a few hours after death has occurred." These goals are ably met. An overview of the funeral industry leads to a description of basic services, the array of "extras," and important facts on cemeteries, vaults, and other coffin enclosures. Embalming procedures are explained by an undertaker, and a list of state embalming laws appears in the appendix. In discussing alternatives to conventional funeral and burial practices, the editors study religious views on cremation, autopsy, and body donation, along with practical and economic considerations. Even though the financial estimates are dated and some of the practices and religious proscriptions may have altered, the book's basic message remains vital: be alert to the possibility of exploitation and be aware of the various options.

Maxwell, Katie. *No Lifetime Guarantee: Dealing with the Details of Death*. 1988. Betterway (P.O. Box 219, Crozet, VA 22932), paper, $9.95.

Maxwell excels at guiding the bereaved through critical funerary, domestic, and ongoing financial decisions. Her matter-of-fact approach calms and informs. Intended as a book to aid widows, Maxwell's guide will benefit any family member facing final arrangements for a loved one. She enumerates the care options for a terminal patient, explains the whys of an autopsy, and describes the procedure for organ donation. Coverage of funeral details is brief, but thorough enough to enable the survivor to ask the right questions. (She also offers a list of fine books on bereavement.) The essence of this guide is financial matters—handling wills, probate, investments, Social Security, estate and inheritance taxes, and credit. Many significant and minor matters are covered here, such as how to face unexpected expenses that may require a loan or sale of personal items. Maxwell has compiled a "survivor's checklist" that cites the decisions that must be made just before and after death, within the first week, second week, and so on. Her book supplies the common sense and impetus many will need to make important decisions.

Nelson, Thomas C. *It's Your Choice: The Practical Guide to Planning a Funeral*. 1983. An AARP Book published for the American Association of Retired Persons by Scott, Foresman; dist. by Little, Brown, paper, $4.95.

Nelson supplies a succinct education in funeral planning. This book's brevity—compared with the Consumer Reports volume—may make it easier to use. The author suggests that individuals plan their own arrangements or consult a legitimate memorial society (the appendix contains a lengthy list of such organizations in the United States and Canada). He warns that the shock or trauma of death may leave a vulnerable decision-maker believing that money spent equals grief felt. Typically a grief-stricken person is not prepared to evaluate costs and services, so he suggests the company of a relative or professional, such as an attorney, during communication with a funeral director. Cost estimates are given (they date, however, from the book's original publication date in 1982). Options for final disposition are clearly outlined. Although Nelson mentions a society for assistance in handling a funeral without a director, no further guidance is provided. (Lisa Carlson covers this topic thoroughly in *Caring for Your Own Dead*, page 52). Fill-in forms to evaluate costs, services, funerals, cemeteries, and monument dealers along with preliminary planning documents appear in the appendix. Most people are unaware of how many details go into planning a funeral: Nelson's book can rectify that deficit.

Loss of Pets

Nieburg, Herbert A., and Arlene Fischer. *Pet Loss: A Thoughtful Guide for Adults and Children.* 1982. Harper, $14.95.
Quackenbush, Jamie, and Denise Graveline. *When Your Pet Dies: How to Cope with Your Feelings.* 1985. Simon & Schuster, $16.95.

Nieburg, a psychotherapist who specializes in grief therapy, was assisted by Fischer, a freelance writer, while Quackenbush, a pet bereavement counselor, was similarly aided by Graveline. The two books differ slightly in tone (Quackenbush presents a warmer, more personal approach) and concentration on a few issues. Overall, either book will be very helpful to those who have lost a beloved pet or who are trying to help a friend or relative cope with such a loss.

Nieburg and Fischer readily explain how the loss of a pet is often downplayed in our society since many people feel they cannot actually mourn an animal, even one that has been a dear friend. Many seniors, like children and adults of all ages, are deeply attached to their pets. When these animals who have "shared our lives, our homes, and our affection" die, a definite sense of loss and need for mourning asserts itself; yet, the inhibitions people feel or have imposed upon them by others will delay or prevent recovery. "Unreleased grief stays with us," the authors warn. Specific suggestions on recognizing the loss and coping with a pet's absence are cited. The range of possibilities for final arrangements, from pet cemeteries or cremation to backyard services or disposal by the veterinarian, are discussed in detail.

Quackenbush and Graveline write more personally. When supplying real-life incidents to demonstrate their advice, they introduce both animals and owners. Emotional aspects more than practical ones are their focus; for example, the information on final arrangements is quite brief. This book contains serious bereavement counseling. The authors describe the anger, guilt, denial, and depression that first hit a bereaved owner. Like Nieburg and Fischer, they discuss the complex emotions aroused by such painful situations as euthanasia, accidental death, runaways, or giving a pet up to a new home or shelter. The sections on helping children cope with the loss of a pet may help grandparents share this experience and guide their families. The book may also aid adult offspring to understand the depth of their parents' feelings and to pursue a sensible path on whether or not to select a new pet. It is nice to see so sensitive a topic covered with precision and compassion.

Travel and Recreation

Here are books on planning and enjoying a safe trip and on filling leisure hours with recreation—both physical and cerebral. The travel guides in the first section carry how-to advice and helpful directions for finding more information. The next section, "Walking, Biking, and Playing," lists titles on some popular activities—card playing, fishing, biking, and golf. It is a small section because, even though there are so many activities a senior can enjoy, few need to be directly channeled. For example, there are a seemingly endless number of fine books on needlework, crafts, and collecting, which are all activities that readily cross age barriers. Joan Heilman's book *Unbelievable Good Deals and Great Adventures* (page 58) is as valuable in planning recreational pursuits as it is for travelers. She notes organizations, tours, and discounts for bikers, skiers, campers, golfers, swimmers, and tennis players, along with addresses for the Over the Hill Gang and the National Senior Sports Association. The NSSA "organizes recreational and competitive tournaments in golf, tennis, bowling, skiing, and fishing at resorts around the country." If you are not a sports buff, other activities described in "Creative Leisure" include staging plays and writing memoirs, poetry, or family history.

Travel Planning

Adler, Jack, and Thomas C. Tompkins. *Travel Safety: Security Safeguards at Home and Abroad*. 1988. Hippocrene, $14.95.

> While this book is not directed specifically at seniors, the advice can certainly be utilized by many older travelers. The authors move beyond the basics of avoiding pickpockets and using traveler's checks to recommendations on how to react to hijackers, burglars, terrorists, muggers, con artists, and fraudulent travel schemes. One chapter is devoted entirely to describing some nifty

travel security devices, including alarms, hidden pockets, locks—even a judo stick key ring. Amazingly, the authors never give the impression that it's better to give up and stay home (although they do suggest ways to secure a house while the occupant is away). The straightforward advice is preceded by realistic scenarios: for example, one man was arrested and severely questioned for attempting a purchase with a credit card that had reached its credit limit. Another couple found that their cruise tickets had been lost or stolen at an airline ticket counter on the first leg of their journey. Common-sense precautions are detailed and, when trouble is unavoidable, the authors explain how to issue a direct appeal to the right authorities.

Barish, Frances. *Frommer's Guide for the Disabled Traveler: United States, Canada, and Europe.* 1984. Frommer/Pasmantier, div. of Simon & Schuster, paper, $10.95.

  The author, a paraplegic, "brings the viewpoint of the permanently seated traveler" to this excellent guide. She offers general planning advice with cues on handling airplane trips and joining tours; however, Louise Weiss in *Access to the World* (page 61) is more comprehensive in this area. Barish's book excels at thorough coverage of specific locales, including seven major U.S. cities (from Washington, D.C., to New Orleans), three Canadian cities, and several European ones (including Amsterdam, Vienna, and Paris). She discusses arrival in each location, major sights (with notes on wheelchair access), restaurants, and recommended accommodations. Maps are supplied for each city and Barish's down-to-earth descriptions for handling the terrain lend an invaluable touch.

Bongartz, Roy, ed. *Travels in America: A Large Print Anthology.* 1988. G. K. Hall Large Print Books, $19.95.

  This selection of nineteen travel essays is a pleasant medley of classics and recent works. Many are not strictly stories but are excerpts from books, among them: *Travels with Charley* by John Steinbeck, *American Fried* by Calvin Trillin, and *Blue Highways* by William Least Heat Moon. Also included is a passage from an anonymous woman's journal written as she traveled westward with a wagon train in the mid-nineteenth century. The locales in these essays vary from Gettysburg to the Los Angeles freeways, and their authors capture the fun, adventure, perils, and especially the spirit of travel. Publishers of books in large print, such as G. K. Hall, often issue compilations like this one along with their ongoing reprinting of popular, current titles. See also the two large-print collections of short stories edited by Mary Allen (page 144).

Dunlop, Richard. *On the Road in an RV.* 1987. An AARP Book published for the American Association of Retired Persons by Scott, Foresman; dist. by Little, Brown, paper, $8.95.

    Citing statistics from an AARP survey, Dunlop states that of thirty million Americans who owned or rented a recreational vehicle (RV) in 1986, nine million were aged fifty years or older. The author focuses his advice on the special needs and interests of seniors who enjoy driving or pulling a home on wheels here and abroad. He explains how to select a suitable, quality vehicle and how an RV can be customized for a traveler with disabilities. A good summary of available equipment from pop-up campers to luxury motor homes is offered. His discussion of the types of camping sites throughout the United States and Canada receives the same breadth of coverage. RV organizations that plan outings, distribute useful maps and guidelines, and set up security measures are discussed. One of these, Loners on Wheels, is made up entirely of single seniors. Trip planning advice includes the basics of map reading (and folding), equipment maintenance, and secure packing. The appendix contains a wealth of further information such as RV clubs, tourist offices, and rental sources. Dunlop provides an ideal introduction to this popular mode of travel.

Heilman, Joan Rattner. *Unbelievable Good Deals and Great Adventures That You Absolutely Can't Get Unless You're over 50.* 1988. Contemporary, paper, $6.95.

    In one convenient resource, nicely designed with slightly larger-than-usual type, are great ways to enhance life—at a discount. While Heilman mentions all sorts of deals that are available for the asking (or the display of a relevant I.D. or membership card), she concentrates on the vast array of travel bargains. Dramatic discounts are offered for golf courses, ski slopes, tennis courts, RV campgrounds, trains, buses, planes, and hotels throughout the world, along with good deals on tax, insurance, restaurants, and shopping. The author highlights the possibilities for group or independent travel, citing such adventurous organizations as the Over the Hill Gang, which plans canoeing, whitewater rafting, skiing, ballooning, surfing, and hiking trips. Travel groups geared exclusively to mature singles will match up cabinmates or roommates, if desired. Along with these terrific travel possibilities, the author reports on opportunities for college courses, pen pals, peer learning programs, beauty pageants, grandparent / grandchild summer camps, bicycling clubs, volunteering, and Senior Olympics. These perks for those over fifty should delight many seniors and certainly stimulate activity whether on the road, in the air, or of the mind.

Hyman, Mildred. *Elderhostels: The Students' Choice.* 1989. John Muir Pr., paper, $12.95.

Elderhostel is the no-credit, high-fun program of education for seniors. Boarding at a college for two or three weeks, a participant can take courses in philosophy, literature, nature studies, sports—just about anything. The classes are described in a newspaper-format bulletin published six or seven times per year. (The address is in the appendix; no membership is required.) There is even a new program involving RV owners. Classes may take place at universities, national parks, music schools, and other meeting centers. This variation adds pleasure and excitement to the experience, but it also results in an unevenness which may distress many seniors. Hyman's book is an attempt to remedy that insecurity. After a few Elderhostel experiences, she realized that the rooms, food, facilities, walkways, and other details are just as significant to seniors as the classes. Her helpful critique focuses on the flaws and fine points of 120 favorites (out of the 1,200 participating universities, colleges, and learning centers throughout the world). The author draws on her own experience, school records, and interviews conducted by a team of sixty-one Elderhostelers, who gathered opinions from students after visits to the most popular locales in the United States, Europe, and the Middle East. Hyman supplies descriptions of teachers, courses, accommodations, food, accessibility, fun quotient, and possible drawbacks in this terrific guide with just the right perspective.

See also the video *Elderhostel* (page 117) and Elderhostel in the Appendix.

Malott, Gene, and Adele Malott. *Get Up and Go: A Guide for the Mature Traveler.* 1989. Gateway Books; dist. by Quality, paper, $10.95.

The Malotts' thorough coverage of all angles of travel is enhanced by their insight on discounts, precautions, and entertainment highlights just for older travelers. Their basics on planning a trip include cues on locating and selectively using a range of sources, including governments, guidebooks, senior and tour groups, and travel agents. In discussing the virtues of each mode of travel—bus, auto, RV, train, plane, and cruise ship—the authors slip in plenty of particulars. For example, there are a dozen great train rides for those over forty-nine and the addresses for several RV clubs. Packing safely, staying healthy, securing the homestead, souvenir shopping, and personal security are a few of the other issues nicely addressed. A section called "Travel Tools" closes each chapter with answers to specific questions on currency conversion, typical climates for spots throughout the world, hotel bargains, and essential travel documents. A family visit or world tour can be plotted with the background provided by the Malotts—there is no excuse to stay home with help like this available.

McMillon, Bill. *Volunteer Vacations: A Directory of Short-term Adventures That Will Benefit You and Others.* Rev. ed. 1989. Chicago Review, paper, $11.95.

Looking for a meaningful, productive vacation? You might find one by volunteering on scientific, ecological, religious, cultural, or construction projects in the United States or abroad. Skilled, trainable, or willing hands are needed for work at national parks, archeological digs, museums, relief centers, railway restoration projects, Indian reservations, and similar sites all over the world. Each page-length description supplies an address and phone number, spells out any required qualifications, and tells about the work and setting. First-hand reports from successful volunteers, interspersed throughout the directory, offer both information and a boost to confidence. One of these is by a "Volunteer Junkie"—a widow who has shared her office skills at retirement centers and nursing facilities across the United States. McMillon's extensive cross-referenced indexes, alphabetized by sponsoring organization, list the jobs by project cost, length, location, season, and type so the prospective volunteer can find just the right avocation vacation.

Webster, Harriet. *Trips for Those over 50.* 1988. Yankee Books, paper, $9.95.

Webster focuses on sights and adventures throughout the New England states of Maine, Vermont, New Hampshire, Massachusetts, and Rhode Island. Her guide opens with a few suggestions especially geared to the older trip-taker on traveling solo, driving, cutting costs, and making careful plans. Sights are geographically sorted, first by state, then by city or area. The author has carefully sought out places that will suit a variety of interests, so that a traveler, or a group, can find plenty to explore during a single journey. The exception, and a worthy one, is the Shaker Village in Canterbury, New Hampshire—a fascinating sight appealing to those whose interests lie in religion, crafts, or history. Flower festivals, concerts, vineyards, racetracks, craft fairs, educational opportunities from birdcarving to studying the classics, historical sites, museums of all sorts, campgrounds, fishing holes, and scenic wonders are samples of the types of activities she has mapped out, complete with directions, addresses, telephone numbers, seasons, and rates. Although no specific schedules are mentioned, the availability of walking, bus, or boat tours is noted. This certainly makes a pleasant guidebook for natives or new visitors to New England, since there is something for everyone.

Weiss, Louise. *Access to the World: A Travel Guide for the Handicapped.* 1983. Facts on File, $16.95; rev. ed., Holt/Owl, paper, $12.95.

    Weiss's guide explains how a permanently or temporarily disabled traveler can journey in comfort and safety. She concentrates on making arrangements and locating essential facts about tours, accommodations, and modes of travel, especially on various airlines and airports. Yet the pros and cons of travel by bus, train, ship, auto, or recreational vehicle are also discussed. General travel tips cover medical care, jet lag, packing efficiently, and traveling solo. Each section contains references for more information. For example, Weiss lists several manufacturers of recreational vehicles that will customize motor homes or trailers. Also supplied is the address for obtaining the international Access Guides list and the U.S. and foreign agencies that will provide these guides as well as other information for the disabled traveler. This reassuring volume should animate even the most wary traveler. See also *Frommer's Guide for the Disabled Traveler* by Frances Barish (page 57).

Wernly, Caroline, and Walter Wernly. *The Discount Guide for Travellers over 55.* 4th ed. 1988. Dutton, paper, $7.95.

    The Wernlys have compiled and regularly update a national discount directory to hotels, motels, restaurants, car rental companies, theaters, museums, and sights throughout the United States. Organized alphabetically by state, then by city, the inclusions are not critically evaluated, but instead discuss specific locations and the level of discounts given to seniors. In their introduction, the authors mention national firms that offer a consistent senior discount and suggest how to seek out the best bargain (some special rates may even offer better savings than the regular discount fare). The authors also discuss other money-saving programs, such as Elderhostel, the national parks passport, and STEPS (Senior

Travel Exchange Program, which involves swapping free board with a European senior). Many senior shoppers, museum-goers, and travelers will find bargains listed in this well-organized guide that they may not have thought to look for.

Walking, Biking, and Playing

Ainslie, Tom. *Tom Ainslie's Complete Hoyle.* 1975. Simon & Schuster, paper, $11.95.

Ainslie offers instruction and a memory refresher on the rules for more than fifty card games. He readily admits that Edwin Hoyle—whose first guide to card playing (on whist) was printed in 1742 when he was age seventy—may have never seen some of these entries. Hoyle's original edition was so successful that he continued to write such guidebooks until his death at ninety-four. Ainslie is admittedly "riding on the old master's coattails . . . just like the makers of dictionaries use the name of Noah Webster." Basic rules from set-up through scoring are clearly explained and illustrated for variations of rummy, poker, solitaire, bridge, and others. More complex games may be found in other sources such as *Goren's Complete Bridge* (Doubleday, 1980, by Charles Goren with Omar Sharif). Ainslie runs through the play of traditional gambling and casino games and supplies rules for popular dice and board games, including chess, checkers, dominoes, Mah-Jongg, backgammon, and Risk. It is always useful to have an authoritative text on hand to establish the rules; but this book could also help calm some of the insecurities of individuals entering a retirement community or social center. The section on children's games will be a great help to grandparents.

Charlton, James, and others. *Croquet: Its History, Strategy, Rules, and Records.* Rev. ed. 1988. Stephen Greene; dist. by Viking, paper, $11.95.

Croquet, a longtime backyard favorite, is an increasingly popular game. This oversized paperback, filled with lively historical information and wonderful illustrations and photographs, is an enticement to become reacquainted with the game. Current practice of croquet ranges from private lawns and amateur leagues to tournament play. Yes, croquet is now recognized as a tournament sport! It is also a fine game for older players (and whenever bending is required yet difficult, the reaching device that helps a person grab an object from a high shelf would spare the back). With wit and fun, the authors detail the specifics on setting up a court, playing, dressing appropriately, achieving tournament status, and playing variations on the game, such as golf croquet and roque. Distinctions between rules and methods of American and British players are also explained. A glossary of game terms and rosters of champions are appended. When looking for a less strenuous alternative to golf—or one more energetic than shuffleboard—one should consider croquet.

Evanoff, Viad. *The Freshwater Fisherman's Bible*. Rev. ed. 1986. Doubleday, paper, $7.95.

Fish by fish, Evanoff tells how to catch them. This unique arrangement, by species rather than a geographical or more specialized guide, makes the book perfect for beginners and casual anglers. Each chapter delineates the habits and habitats of over thirty common North American fish. General notes on which rivers and waters each species inhabits lead into specifics on how they congregate and travel. In a comfortable, chatty style, he reports the most effective bait, typical size, preferred temperatures, and the difficulty level for catching each species. While Evanoff can describe a fish in three or four pages, the acclaimed fishing expert Ernest Schwiebert required 1,745 pages to discuss his favorite fish in *Trout* (Dutton, 1978). Schwiebert has also written a wonderful portrait of a traditional expedition featuring his grown son, ninety-year-old father, and himself in *A River for Christmas*, a collection of his classic fishing stories.

Evanoff also offers some basics on rods and reels, peppered with precautions on knowing the style of fishing intended before buying any costly equipment. Whether to identify what you've caught or to check what fish are running in nearby waters, at home or on vacation this book is a handy fishing tool.

Player, Gary, with Desmond Tolhurst. *Golf Begins at 50: Playing the Lifetime Game Better than Ever*. 1988. Simon & Schuster, $18.95.

Player, who joined the Senior Tour in 1985 and won several championships, redefines the game for older players. He has developed a "walk-through swing" that protects the back and gives greater power. His stroke, grip adjustment, and stance are thoroughly explained in words, drawings, and photographs. Player's techniques can help golfers reserve strength and adjust their play to their own body's telling messages. He moves through an entire game, guiding a golfer through the fairways, traps, and greens and the variety of strokes required at each. Player's best advice is: "Don't become a grouch on the golf course . . . enjoy your game, have fun! You'll play better." One definite way to feel and play better, insists this South African championship golfer, is by staying fit. He supports yoga as enthusiastically as golf. Player supplies an illustrated run-through of his own exercise regime, frequently citing how much of it is based on yoga routines and relaxation. He mentions how unfortunate it is that this ancient "system designed to give you the ultimate in physical and mental fitness" has been "mistrusted in the West as an occult Eastern practice." Perhaps his pep talk on conditioning and sensible eating will convince those golfers who won't listen to Richard Simmons or anyone else. With attention given to relaxation and fitness Player promises, "Life, as well as golf, will be far more fun."

Skillman, Don, and Lolly Skillman. *Pedaling Across America.* 1988. Velo-News, paper, $9.95.

Don, Lolly, and Don's brother Bill rode their bicycles more than 4,000 miles from Neskowin, Oregon, to Virginia Beach, Virginia. Their combined age was 153 years. The trio often biked long distances along the Pacific Northwest coast, and plans for this book's adventure first emerged as a fantasy during one of their journeys. Traveling in May, they had hoped for ideal weather; instead, they were forced to backtrack over 100 miles when their path through Yellowstone Park was closed by a severe snowstorm (at one point they biked past skiers). Don narrates their thrilling journey in this edited version of their journals. He tells how the trio polished off mountains of pancakes (essential for the readily burned carbohydrates) to the amazement of café waitresses and diners. He also recalls scary punctures, incredibly nice people (and a share of rude ones), and, especially, the rigors of pedaling long distances every day (an average of sixty to seventy-five miles with eight hours in the seat). They arrived in Virginia Beach after fifty-six days. Along with maps, there is an appendix containing practical notes on conditioning, equipment, repairs, safety, and costs. A British grandmother, Christian Miller, wrote a charming book about her biking adventures across America entitled *Daisy, Daisy* (Doubleday, 1981).

Sussman, Aaron, and Ruth Goode. *The Magic of Walking.* 1980. Simon & Schuster, O.P.

Here is a fun, informative volume perfect for an armchair

read or pre-stroll inspiration. The advisory essays opening the book are written in a mellow tone, yet they thoroughly explain how walking suits the design of the human body, benefits the heart, and can serve as a non-dieter's diet. The how-to's of pace, distance, wardrobe, and shoes are covered. A state-by-state directory of places to walk includes beaches, forest preserves, parks, towpaths, and famous hiking trails. Finally there is a lovely selection of poetry, stories, and excerpted prose from such authors as G. K. Chesterton, John Muir, and Ray Bradbury. An annotated bibliography describes books so enticing that they may tempt too many walkers from the path to the reading chair. Several of the books described are of a practical nature on topics such as bird watching, rock collecting, and city walking tours. These essays share the pleasure of walking in cities, mountains, beaches, parks, or just around the block. This may be just the volume to convince reluctant walkers who are put off by the fitness-or-else approach of Elaine LaLanne's *Dynastride* (page 26) and similar guides.

See also *Unbelievable Good Deals and Great Adventures*, by Joan Heilman (page 58) for plenty of ideas on biking, camping, tennis, skiing, golfing, and swimming. See also books on exercise (yoga, swimming, and walking) listed in the Health chapter. Check the note on the video *Richard Simmons and the Silver Foxes* (page 119).

Creative Leisure

Arthur, Stephen, and Julia Arthur. *Your Life and Times: How to Put a Life Story on Tape—An Oral History Handbook*. 1987. Genealogical Pub., paper, $8.95.

The Arthurs open their book with an intriguing question: "Can you imagine what it would be like to actually hear the voice of your great-great-grandparents speaking to you?" Assuming an affirmative reaction, the authors explain how to provide that opportunity for future generations. To begin with, the Arthurs suggest digging out photo albums, scrapbooks, family letters, documents, and any other memorabilia as a source of inspiration. This guide is filled with such basic questions as, "Do I remember any favorite toys, playthings, or family pets from my earliest days?" The authors even give cues to begin the taping, such as, "My name is _____. I was born in _____." Terse but useful instructions on audiotaping are given. If the prospect of facing an audio (or video) tape recorder is too daunting, the Arthurs suggest compiling the answers to their leading questions (and the resulting flood of memories) in a notebook. The arrangement is chronological, starting with place of birth and family days through education, work experience, and retirement. The questions presuppose a stereotyped life experience and those who have faced many crises may be annoyed at the blithesome tone of the questions. Still, their idea is a good one, and the sheer volume of questions should trigger many memories that a self-directed memoir could miss.

Bonsey, Lynn, and Lorna Healey. *It's All Relative: How to Create Your Own Personal Family History Trivia Game.* 1988. Heritage Books (1540E Pointer Ridge Place, Bowie, MD 20716), paper, $9.95.

These sisters created a personal trivia game based upon their family history as a gift for their parents. This delightful idea seems to have been a spin-off of the popular board game Trivial Pursuit. The authors clearly define how to establish categories and organize the game. They explain how to create a family tree that is useful for compiling questions as well as organizing interviews. They discuss how to sift through family and public records. This research angle takes up most of the book, and can be helpful to any family archivist. The sisters also share many of their own general questions that are transferable. The questions range from the zany ("Who ate three Big Macs in ten minutes?") to the historical ("How much was a Hershey bar in 1963?"). This unique way to explore one's roots is a great suggestion for a retiree in need of an entertaining project or for a gift to an older relative.

Fischer, Edward. *Life in the Afternoon: Good Ways of Growing Older.* 1987. Paulist Pr., $8.95.

In a pleasant yet stern fashion, Fischer offers lessons on accepting aging and filling retirement years with contentment and significance. "When suddenly released from the restraints that go with making a living, you need imagination and discipline to impose on yourself a new outlook," Fischer notes. "Without a new vocation you might find yourself surviving rather than living." He stresses that simple busyness is not recommended, and that a new sense of purpose is essential. His specific suggestions on continuing to grow and mature may be familiar—volunteer work, education, new friendships, travel, exercise, and reading. Infused with his personal religious faith (without preaching) and experience, Fischer's writing results in a serious yet amusing, anecdote-filled discussion. This is a book that concerned adult offspring can pass along to their parents if they seem to have hit the doldrums. Fischer speaks forthrightly against the cantankerousness and outright laziness of many of his peers while offering some sage antidotes to such behavior.

Koch, Kenneth. *I Never Told Anybody: Poetry Writing in a Nursing Home.* 1977. Random, O.P.

Koch, a talented poet and professor at Columbia University, taught a poetry-writing and appreciation course to residents of the American Nursing Home in New York City. His students were modestly educated and did not necessarily have a literary background. Through a series of sixteen weekly workshops, Koch familiarized his elderly audience with poetry, a genre once thought remote and unknown. He found it heartening to observe the novices' growing affection for words and their abilities at self-expression. Koch taught that everyone has poetry within herself or himself and may write, even if not for publication. It should be remembered, though, that fame is not an impossibility for a nursing home author. Consider the resounding success of octogenarian Helen Santmyer's novel . . . *And Ladies of the Club* (page 132).

Steward, Joyce S., and Mary K. Croft. *The Leisure Pen: A Book for Elderwriters.* 1988. Keepsake (P.O. Box 21; Plover, WI 54467), paper, $10.95.

Steward and Croft cite several ways in which writing can enrich an older person's life. Their book is a gentle nudge toward journal-keeping, creating a memoir or family history, or writing for publication. Several people who have participated in the authors' seminars share the pleasure and satisfaction achieved by writing. They speak of it as therapy for grief or depression, as a means of community involvement (beginning with letters to the editor), and as a satisfying method of passing on a legacy of family facts and lore. There are some recommendations on composing poetry, stories, and nonfiction for the marketplace, but such advice can be found in greater detail in other writers' guides (Kenneth Koch writes about composing poetry in *I Never Told Anybody*, above). Suggestions on establishing a comfortable writing niche and a regular routine are included with other ideas that will give inspiration and momentum to a beginner. This book's charm and value lie in its reassurances that everyone can and should share his or her reflections in writing.

Vorenberg, Bonnie L., ed. *New Plays for Mature Actors: An Anthology.*
1987. Coach House Pr. (P.O. Box 458, Morton Grove, IL 60053),
$19.95.

The ten plays selected for this anthology are the work of
new playwrights who display "a lively, positive view of aging."
Vorenberg explains in her introduction that she sought sensible
scripts with non-complicated settings and a majority of women's
roles. One other feature was "a good sense of logic to aid in memori-
zation." The brief one- and two-act plays are thematically arranged
under chapter titles: "New Challenges," "Stories of Adventure," "Intergenerational Connections," and "Love Resolved." They are delightful—an array of espionage, romance, comedy, and drama. Am-
ateurs who enjoy readings or performances will relish this volume
(royalty information is provided), produced under the auspices of
the National Center on Arts and Aging, a program of the National
Council on Aging. More widely known plays that touch upon issues
concerning aging are cited in Chapter 11.

See also *Write Stories to Me, Grandpa!*, by Meyer Moldeven
(page 17); *Starting a Mini-Business: A Guidebook for Seniors,* by
Nancy Olsen (page 80); the chapter Plays and Films; and the Elderhostel listing in the Appendix.

Chapter 6

Housing

One of the first things many people consider when they plan their retirement is moving to a new residence, either in a designated senior citizens' area or a treasured vacation spot. The guides in this chapter cover both early decisions and the later ones that may become necessary due to changing health or other needs. Actually, many people who ponder their own retirement housing requirements are also active in the planning of their parents' moves to nursing homes or similar increased care facilities. These issues are discussed along with the vital matters of home and personal security.

Home Ownership and Relocation

Boyer, Richard, and David Savageau. *Retirement Places Rated: All You Need to Plan Your Retirement.* 1988. Prentice-Hall, paper, $14.95.

Boyer and Savageau have rated 131 locations on how well each meets standards for six basic needs: money, climate, safety, services, housing, and leisure living. The general term "place" is used deliberately because counties have been evaluated even though areas may be pinpointed on specific graphs by the best-known city in the vicinity. Murray–Kentucky Lake, Kentucky, received the best marks overall, while Portsmouth–Dover–Durham, New Hampshire, received the worst. However, by looking at how an area rates in each particular category, retirees (present or potential) may make their judgments weighted by which issue is most significant. The book can lead you to the lowest utility rates, the most libraries or championship bowling alleys, or the shortest ragweed season, to name only a few of the numerous factors compared. Yet this is not just a book of numbers: additional information and helpful tips are also included, such as using an Elderhostel pro-

gram to rehearse living in an area. Although limited in scope, this book suggests places to relocate beyond the common Arizona or Florida market and demonstrates the variety of issues to be considered.

Carlin, Vivian F., and Ruth Mansberg. *If I Live to Be 100: A Creative Housing Solution for Older People.* 2nd ed. 1989. Princeton Book Co. (P.O. Box 57, Pennington, NJ 08534), paper, $14.95.

    This book was originally intended as a "survey of several types of residential communities . . . but, soon focused on just one— a middle-income congregate residence that seemed to epitomize a communal lifestyle for older Americans." The authors' enthusiasm is readily understandable since this increasingly popular housing option offers communal services (dining, health care, and transportation) as well as independent living in a private apartment. Many older citizens, especially those beyond the first decade of retirement, are choosing such a lifestyle. Carlin lived in one of these residences on and off for more than three years in order to glean the style, spirit, and effectiveness of the place. Her research has resulted in an engaging, first-person summary of the advantages and possible drawbacks to congregate housing. A state-by-state list of life care congregate communities throughout the United States (complete with addresses and phone numbers) is a helpful addendum and has been updated for this second edition. A final chapter touches upon alternative living situations, but these authors did a more thorough job on this subject in *Where Can Mom Live? A Fam-*

ily Guide to Living Arrangements for Elderly Parents (reviewed below).

Carlin, Vivian F., and Ruth Mansberg. *Where Can Mom Live? A Family Guide to Living Arrangements for Elderly Parents.* 1987. Lexington Books, paper, $12.95.

Carlin and Mansberg address the relatives rather than the older individuals themselves who must change their current lifestyle for health, financial, or personal reasons. Their suggestions range from house-sharing among peers to life care communities; they also "touch on other alternatives, such as living with adult children, retirement villages, residential hotels, elder cottages, and board-and-care homes." By sharing actual experiences of several families, the authors lend a warm, personal approach to such decision-making. Specific suggestions are offered for tactfully introducing the topic of a new residence when the older individual does not take the initiative. Handy checklists designed for guiding the parent to the appropriate move or for establishing a more secure environment if the decision is made to stay at home are included. The appendix contains addresses and phone numbers of helpful agencies and organizations.

Gold, Margaret. *Guide to Housing Alternatives for Senior Citizens.* 1985. Consumer Reports Books, paper, $9.95.

The Consumers Union, so helpful when it's time to select a new car or appliance, offered another practical service when they investigated a wealth of housing alternatives for retirees. Retirement communities in the Sunbelt and throughout the United States receive thorough coverage. Other options are explored, including staying in a familiar house or area, or sharing a home with peers or relatives. The familiar decision to live with adult offspring is delivered with some new twists as Gold explains how independence may be maintained through in-law suites or echo housing (a small residence built on the same property). Guidance is also given on the selection of nursing homes. Beyond the general pros and cons of each option, Gold details relevant technical and legal ramifications along with sources for further information. This well-thought-out guide can help individuals planning an immediate or future move and enlighten adult offspring who must assist their parents in such decisions.

Hayes, Nan DeVincentis. *Move It! A Guide to Relocating Family, Pets, and Plants.* 1989. Dembner Books; dist. by Norton, paper, $11.95.

Hayes attempts to eliminate the stress and confusion of moving with this handy, step-by-step guide. Even though her emphasis is on moving a family, there are plenty of tips for older couples or singles. The section on moving pets is particularly helpful. In the opening chapter, she offers a "should-I-move?" quiz that even the determined relocater ought to consider. Home sale and purchase are briefly covered, along with some good suggestions for maintaining security in an empty house. Her instructions on taking inventory combine a number of time-consuming steps, including deciding what to keep, evaluating the costs of repair and cleaning, planning a garage sale, and noting values for insurance purposes. Sources listed for further information range from moving companies to the IRS. Hayes details the pros and cons of crucial decisions such as using a moving company and selling through a realtor. This is a comforting, informative book for people overwhelmed at the prospect of packing and relocating.

Horne, Jo, and Leo Baldwin. *Homesharing and Other Lifestyle Options.* 1987. An AARP Book published for the American Association of Retired Persons by Scott, Foresman; dist. by Little, Brown, $12.95.

Horne and Baldwin enthusiastically outline the possibilities and realities of homesharing. They speak directly to older individuals who are seeking a middle ground between retirement villages and nursing homes. Homesharing can offer privacy, security, financial stability, autonomy, companionship, and as much care (or as little) as needed. The authors explain how group homes can be (and have been) developed independently or by an organization, church group, or government agency. They explain in detail how to find the right people to offer advice, do the work, and share the housing. Matters such as expenses, contracts, residents' backgrounds, and attendants' qualifications must be thoroughly assessed. Other housing options, covered in less detail, are echo housing, accessory apartments, board-and-care homes, and congregate housing (more thoroughly covered in Carlin and Mansberg's books in this section). The authors' use of real-life situations to demonstrate how decisions can be agreeably reached is appealing, but sometimes Pollyanna-ish. Some suggestions are made to relatives faced with assisting in these decisions, but mostly the older individual is spoken to directly. This attitude is an important plus in a field where so many books are written about and at—but rarely to—the most significant audience, the older reader.

Raper, Ann Trueblood, and Anne C. Kalicki, eds. *National Continuing Care Directory: Retirement Communities with Nursing Care.* 2nd ed. 1988. An AARP Book published for the American Association of Retired Persons by Scott, Foresman; dist. by Little, Brown, $19.95.

Continuing Care Retirement Communities (CCRCs) span the gap between a retirement condo and a nursing home. They supply long-term housing and nursing care typically under a contractual agreement that provides the institution up-front funding (in the form of a large down payment) and assures the individual of ongoing medical attention if serious illness strikes. This means that a person or couple who contracts to live in a CCRC pays an admission fee as well as monthly rent, that differs according to the care required.

In the introduction, the variances in financial, residence, and care agreements are defined, as are federal and state restrictions and regulations. For evaluating such housing, a consumer checklist is included along with further suggestions and warnings on selecting an appropriate residence or care facility. A special features index cites additional conveniences and attributes; these can help an individual decide upon a residence by qualities other than location. This directory is arranged by state, then alphabetically by name of the residence.

The American Association of Homes for the Aging (AAHA) is a trade organization for nonprofit housing, health-related facilities, and community services for the elderly. The AAHA (not affiliated with the AARP) developed this guide, which describes 366

CCRCs throughout the United States. Each one-page description lists an abundance of information, including the essentials on fees, notes on the sizes and types of the buildings (i.e., apartments, condos, residential housing), degree of medical and nutritional care, financial plans, date opened, population figures, and the existence of a waiting list.

See also *Every Day Is SUNDAY* by Ralph Schoenstein (page 99).

Nursing Homes

Bausell, R. Barker, and others. *How to Evaluate and Select a Nursing Home.* 1988. Addison-Wesley, paper, $7.95.
Nassau, Jean Baron. *Choosing a Nursing Home.* 1975. Funk & Wagnalls, O.P.

These guides offer excellent direction in finding the right nursing care facility. They differ more in tone than in quality or content. Both explain types of facilities available, essential licensing, and payment methods, and describe how a nursing home should look, operate, and be staffed. Bausell also covers alternatives that have developed over the past few years, while Nassau cites the essential issues to discuss and questions to ask. Bausell supplies detailed charts of these concerns, including a convenient checklist for photocopying that allows onsite completion and comparison. If the decision remains difficult, a mathematical formula is suggested. Although it seems colder, Bausell's book is easier to use. Other charts evaluate a potential patient's financial status so that the most reasonable facility can be sought. While using Bausell's charts and checklists, it would still be feasible to use Nassau's more personal, compassionate approach. She frequently reminds the reader to involve the patient, even if his or her understanding is limited. She also explains the workings of a utilization review board which may expel a resident whose needs have grown too serious (or improved too much) for continued care at the nursing home level. Her thoughtful chapter on how to handle admission day is particularly helpful. These two indispensable guides can simplify a most difficult decision.

Horne, Jo. *The Nursing Home Handbook: A Guide for Families.* 1989. An AARP Book published for the American Association of Retired Persons by Scott, Foresman; dist. by Little, Brown, paper, $9.95.

Horne tries to remove the panic from the term "nursing home"—words which "strike fear, or at least dread in the hearts of older persons and their family members and friends." Her calm, reasoned approach helps mute the trauma while providing practical assistance to individuals who must locate and assess nursing home facilities. She writes for the caregiver, because entry into a nursing home is often immediately necessary, either for convalescence or in cases where the patient is too frail for continued home care. She explains how to handle emergency placement, from evaluating nursing home care and conditions to applying for Medicaid assistance. She spells out in greater detail how to prescreen by telephone and then take an informed tour. Her checklists can help an interviewee raise critical questions without embarrassment, interview staff members, and note details that may blur when several residences are under consideration. Throughout the assessment procedure, she suggests keeping the patient as involved as possible. Some particularly thoughtful suggestions are included for moving day, visits, and special shared activities. Horne also discusses the caregiver's emotional adjustment and mentions positive steps for correcting minor and major complaints. Her suggestions for improving nursing homes in general, through extended community and family involvement, are well worth heeding.

Rossi, Ted. *Step by Step: How to Actively Ensure the Best Possible Care for Your Aging Relative.* 1987. Warner, paper, $9.95.

Rossi's guide primarily covers selecting and maintaining quality nursing home care for an elderly relative or friend, although alternatives are discussed, including in-home services, adult day-care programs, residential care homes, hospices, and respite care. Respite care takes place at nursing homes or private care centers and offers the family time to take a vacation or make other arrangements. Compared with the other guides in this section, Rossi's selection of information is not as extensive. However, he excels at offering suggestions to ease the trauma of moving day and enrich the person's life once she or he is settled. The Patient's Bill of Rights is reprinted and several ways to monitor the quality of nursing home care are suggested. Also included are a short glossary of medical terms often used in nursing homes and a brief discussion of significant legal concerns. This book will definitely help sustain a family when nursing home care is required.

Tisdale, Sallie. *Harvest Moon: Portrait of a Nursing Home.* 1987. Holt, $17.45.

Tisdale, a registered nurse, has experience in a variety of nursing homes and hospitals. She has carefully observed and worked in one small, nonprofit nursing home in order to write this book. For the sake of privacy she created pseudonyms for the patients, staff, and institution, which she calls Harvest Moon. Rather than an exposé, her book is a detailing of the very "ordinary, even familial things that happen here." She shares the routines, harmony, and pain of living and working in such an environment. The personalities, gripes, and more inspired moments of the diverse staff are depicted. Introductions to several patients demonstrate the range of problems—social, physical, sexual, and emotional— that must be solved to maintain quality care and a peaceful environment. Tisdale's compassion and nursing skills are evident in her blend of information and insight. She capably moves from management concerns (for example, considering what advantages this small home may have over a residence that is part of a profit-making conglomerate) to the regrets and worries of a single, aging woman. This earnest insider's view can assist people who are considering nursing home care. Tisdale demonstrates that the decision requires far more than simply ticking off a list of preferred features.

See also *The Age Care Sourcebook,* by Jean Crichton (page 4), and the section Assisting Aging Parents (pages 19–23).

Security and Personal Safety

Geiger, Richard H. *Protect Your Home: A Commonsense Guide to Home Security.* 1987. Storey Communications/Garden Way (Schoolhouse Rd., Pownal, VT 05261), $8.95.

Geiger focuses exclusively and extensively on the technology of burglar alarm systems. He insists that a loud, distinctive-sounding siren, bell, or alarm accompanied by bright lights is the best deterrent to a home intruder. He also includes descriptions of silent systems that directly alert authorities. For those unable to afford even the least expensive system, he suggests a very primitive but functional home-made version that involves a clothespin, popsicle stick, and buzzer. Geiger discusses guns and guard dogs seriously but recommends: "don't purchase a dog for protection." He gives some eye-opening warnings on how landscaping can aid a thief. Geiger mentions the hiding places typically used for valuables, offering some clever alternatives, and stresses the need for an exhaustive household inventory to supply evidence in case of fire or theft. The final chapter consists of fill-in-the-blank forms with names of typical items found in each room along with plenty of space for specific descriptions. This entire guide should help seniors rethink the safety of their current home or plan safely for a new one.

Persico, J. E., with George Sunderland. *Keeping Out of Crime's Way: The Practical Guide for People over 50.* 1985. An AARP Book published for the American Association of Retired Persons by Scott, Foresman; dist. by Little, Brown, paper, $6.95.

This lively report explains how to avoid crooks, con artists, and quacks. Lessons on how not to be a victim of street crime, mail fraud, theft, travel scams, and other illicit doings are presented without condescension. The authors reveal the basics on burglar-proofing a car and house (advice on the latter can be found in greater detail in Richard Geiger's *Protect Your Home,* above). Common swindles such as unnecessary home repairs, phone calls from a phony bank examiner, mail order real estate deals, or bogus health cures (especially for arthritis, cancer, hearing loss) are thoroughly described. By citing typical instances of fraud, along with such physical dangers as robbery, rape, and assault, the authors demand that older victims, especially, take these matters with due seriousness. The guide ends on an optimistic note with suggestions on anti-crime measures for citizens. As in Geiger's book, lessons are given on listing all possessions, and blank space is provided to accomplish the job.

See also *Travel Safety,* by Jack Adler and Thomas C. Tompkins (page 56).

Chapter 7

Retirement: Legal and Financial Planning

Many people will turn directly to this chapter for resources on relocation, retirement hot spots, and so on; however, books on these specific
topics are found in Chapter 6 under Home Ownership and Relocation
(pages 69–74). The books discussed here focus on jobs, money, and the
law. The first section covers retirement planning, compulsory unem-
ployment, and creative second careers. These are followed by books
that explain the legal rights of senior citizens and what recourse to
pursue when those rights are not honored. In the next section are
guides on financial planning suitable for adults of all ages, including
books on living wills, wills, trusts, and estate planning. This chapter
concludes with information on the Social Security system and Medicare.

Retirement and Employment

Brudney, Juliet F., and Hilda Scott. *Forced Out: When Veteran Employees Are Driven from Their Careers.* 1987. Simon & Schuster,
$16.95; paper, $7.95.

Brudney and Scott issue stern warnings on the prevalence
of age discrimination in today's job market but offer sound advice
on combating this threat. They interviewed more than one hundred
people between the ages of fifty and seventy who "believed in the
American Dream . . . that if you work hard, show initiative, don't
make too many waves, and save your money you will progress up
the ladder." Yet many men and women have been pushed off that
ladder. Suddenly they lost their supposedly secure mid-level jobs
because companies wanted younger employees whose salaries
would be lower or wanted to avoid paying promised retirement ben-

efits. In no-nonsense terms, the authors explain how to recognize the warning signs for such discrimination and obtain evidence necessary to convince the EEOC (Equal Employment Opportunities Commission) that the Age Discrimination Act has been violated. Their advice goes far beyond legal recourse, and they offer suggestions on job-hunting in a discriminatory market by offering tactics as well as resources. These resources include state agencies, job fairs, employment counselors, networking, want ads, and nonprofit services. The authors present a glimpse of harsh reality—not many older workers who are fired or forced to retire can regain a position similar to the one they lost: "The older job hunter carries an invisible stigma along with the visible gray hairs." Still there is hope and there are methods, both of which are ably shared in this guide.

Ellison, James W., and others. *Retiring on Your Own Terms: Your Total Retirement Planning Guide to Finances, Health, Life-style, and Much, Much More.* 1989. Crown, $16.95.

This well-written guide is based upon a Pre-Retirement Education Program (PREP) launched at the Columbia Broadcasting System (CBS) in 1981. The authors begin with investment advice then offer suggestions for filling the retirement years with good health and satisfying activities. Using a single woman and a married couple as models, the authors specifically outline how to estimate current financial status and potential retirement income. One valuable suggestion is for people to experiment with living on retirement income in order to judge how comfortable it will be. Investment opportunities for immediate and long-range planning are spelled out. General health and nutrition suggestions are covered. The authors announce that upon retirement most people will suddenly be given a "gift of time" lasting at least 43,680 hours per year. They insist that retirees structure this time so that possibilities for further education, volunteerism, and travel can be explored. However, new jobs are most enthusiastically endorsed. They tell of former high-ranking CBS employees who now happily peddle popcorn from a street stand, gift-wrap at Bloomingdales, and make sandwiches at a deli: "If we can overcome obstacles of ego we might not consider it beneath our dignity to work at a job that is not as high on the ladder as our previous position. Work takes on an entirely different meaning when you don't have to carve out a career."

Goodman, Eugene B. *All the Justice I Could Afford.* 1983. Harcourt, $16.95.

In 1972 at age fifty-four, Goodman joined the Heublein Corporation as director of marketing, with promises of a substantial salary increase and promotion to a vice presidency within a year. Instead he received six years of painful litigation over age discrimination. Shortly after he was hired, the company headed into a youth-oriented management policy in which deliberate down-scaling and elimination of older employees was forcefully encouraged. Goodman's promised promotion—and his entire department—evaporated. From the moment Goodman made his first inquiry to the Department of Labor over possible age discrimination, Heublein's legal forces attacked. He writes with a keening sense of injustice over the legal machinations that resulted in sixteen days in court and a jury-mandated award of over $400,000. Yet this initial victory was short-lived. Heublein refused to pay and continued appeals over another three years. Finally, when his own attorneys began demanding a considerable salary increase, Goodman (still unemployed) represented himself. He appeared *pro se* in the U.S. Court of Appeals for the Second Circuit before a panel of judges who accepted the initial jury verdict but rescinded a later payment of interest for the time since the original award. Goodman's own verdict is: "Justice was done so far as damages for what had happened to me. Justice was not done by the court, however, so far as considering what an aborted career is worth in an American court of law under the Age Statute."

Olsen, Nancy. *Starting a Mini-Business: A Guidebook for Seniors.* 2nd ed. 1988. Fair Oaks (941 Populus Pl., Sunnyvale, CA 94086), paper, $8.95.

Encouraging words and practical advice are offered by Olsen, an experienced counselor for seniors. She stresses the sense of satisfaction, both monetary and personal, that can result from forming a successful, needed mini-business in a local community. Olsen defines how an individual can realize which of his or her interests, skills, and hobbies could be turned into a practical and profitable pastime. The possibilities range from baking bread to toy repair, as well as more conventional jobs. Olsen does not list suggestions, but mentions several other books that do. Her approach is supportive—without being overly optimistic—and always practical. She thoroughly spells out the proper steps from initial brainstorming and customer research to handling licensing, taxes, and zoning questions. Further help can be sought from the many books, organizations, and government agencies that are cited throughout this helpful resource.

See also *The Senior Citizen's Handbook,* by Wesley J. Smith (page 8) and the two sections Walking, Biking, and Playing and Creative Leisure (pages 62–68) for books on filling retirement days with enjoyment and activity.

Legal Affairs

Brown, Robert N., and others. *The Rights of Older Persons.* 2nd ed. 1988. Southern Illinois Univ. Pr., paper, $7.95.

Brown's coauthors are the Legal Counsel for the Elderly, a division of the American Association of Retired Persons (AARP). Because this book was published within a series titled "American Civil Liberties Union Handbooks," the focus differs from the AARP publication *Your Legal Rights in Later Life,* by John J. Regan (page 82). The ACLU's province is defined as "freedom of inquiry and expression, due process of law, equal protection of the laws, and privacy." Few concerns mentioned here fall outside of these specific guidelines. Three significant areas are explored: the right to an adequate income, the right to health care, and the right to freedom from restraints on life, liberty, and property. The discussions on Social Security, retirement income, and job discrimination in the first two sections are valuable. Questions on Medicare, Medicaid, and civil rights within a nursing home and hospital are also answered. In the final section concerns are addressed regarding the appointment of guardians and conservators, commitment hearings and procedures, emergency detention for mental or physical illness, and the right to refuse medical treatment. Older citizens and their advocates can better protect their benefits, safety, and well-being with an awareness of relevant laws, court decisions, and government-agency regulations that are provided here. One drawback to this guide is its small paperback size and small print.

The Reader's Digest Legal Question and Answer Book. 1988. Reader's Digest Pr.; dist. by Random, $25.98.

Editors from *Reader's Digest* consulted with the national firm Hyatt Legal Services to compile this useful resource. It is a good overview of such subjects as consumer rights, property agreements, financial concerns, and marital and childcare issues. The book is not directed solely at any age group, nor does it advocate a do-it-yourself program. After all, older citizens encounter every sort of legal question from child custody (or grandparents' rights) to starting a business. The question-and-answer format, coupled with the no-nonsense, straightforward language, results in a helpful, accessible resource. Along with direct questions and answers, lengthier passages explain matters such as the steps in a divorce, health insurance selection, government rules regarding pension plans, the pros and cons of condominium ownership, and other matters too critical or complex to be condensed into a brief response. Certainly not intended to assume the place of an attorney, the book can help a citizen recognize when legal counsel is needed, what issues need to be addressed, and how to select capable representation.

Regan, John J. *Your Legal Rights in Later Life.* 1988. An AARP Book published for the American Association of Retired Persons by Scott, Foresman; dist. by Little, Brown, paper, $13.95.

Regan is a law professor who has worked closely with AARP's Legal Counsel for the Elderly (LCE) to create this specialized guide. Many of the questions that Regan addresses have been directed by seniors in Pennsylvania to LCE's state hotline over the past few years. The actual questions are printed and answered directly after the relevant sections of legal information. This technique provides a quick source for a specific query as well as a practical reinforcement of the ideas already introduced. The essentials—such as retirement income sources, including Social Security, railroad benefits, and veterans' benefits—and relevant federal tax laws, are well-covered. Home ownership and sale are analyzed, as are rental situations from the perspective of both landlord and tenant. Only a brief consideration of grandparents' rights appears in the section on family law, which also covers marriage contracts and parental abuse. Besides basics on estate planning and wills, there is an entire chapter titled "Planning for Future Incapacity" (including sample forms for a living will and the power of attorney for health care). This book not only addresses matters particularly important to older citizens, but it is also written directly and straightforwardly to them. The wide margins and quite readable print are other assets.

Sloan, Irving J. *The Right to Die: Legal and Ethical Problems.* 1988. Oceana, $10.00.

Sloan seeks to clarify the "complex matrix of rights, duties, and responsibilities that govern the doctor-patient relationship, especially in the context of the terminally ill." In his review of relevant legal and judicial decrees, the author has made some complicated material accessible on this difficult issue. Sloan traces the evolution of social thought on the right to die. References include cases of euthanasia, abortion, suicide, refusal to cease life-support systems, and terminating life-support systems. Sloan describes the controversy surrounding the Uniform Rights of the Terminally Ill Act (a complete copy is included). The appendix contains a chart highlighting the significant provisions of each state's Living Will Act. Also appended are statements from the American Medical Association and the Catholic Church. Not strictly for lawyers or legislators, Sloan's resource can help the individual make important personal decisions and call for political action.

See also *Terminal Choices* by Robert N. Wennberg, page 47.

Financial Planning, Wills, and Trusts

Esperti, Robert, and Renno L. Peterson. *Loving Trust: The Right Way to Provide for Yourself and Guarantee the Future of Your Loved Ones.* 1988. Viking, $19.95.

The authors open their book by vilifying lawyers, bankers, life insurance agents, and others who have drawn up wills, set property in joint tenancy, and performed similar, seemingly appropriate legal acts. Such a dramatic introduction is intended to make their point that these systems lead to probate, can cause difficulties in managing property for the disabled, and otherwise entangle financial control of an estate. The system recommended by these two attorneys is called a living trust—a contract which, like a will, offers instructions on property distribution upon death. Unlike a will, it becomes active before death so that a designated trustee can handle funds for care in case of a long-term physical problem. It can also specify the amounts and times certain bequests should be bestowed. The practical means for devising such a trust are spelled out with cautious warnings about consulting a professional so that legal terms, forms, and signatures are incorporated. A living trust is not a do-it-yourself project. The authors offer their address for inquiries in case knowledgeable, professional help is unavailable. With such potential entanglements as disabling illness, remarriage and stepchildren, and financial investments, this book should be considered.

Hughes, Theodore, and David Klein. *A Family Guide to Wills, Funerals, and Probate: How to Protect Yourself and Your Survivors.* (Paperback revision of *A Family Guide to Estate Planning, Funeral*

Arrangements, and Settling an Estate after Death, 1983). 1987. Scribners, $13.95.

As the original title of the hardcover edition implies, this guide covers the transfer of assets to survivors, as well as final disposition of the body. The first half contains recommendations for sorting out personal affairs; succinct explanations of wills, trusts, probate, death taxes, living wills, and letters of instruction are delivered. An especially interesting section explains what a will cannot or should not do, debunking myths that have been popularized in fiction and on television. The remainder of the book addresses survivors of the deceased. For them, the authors discuss handling final arrangements, locating the will, and participating in its enactment. A nice sorting-out of a difficult issue that lends direction in performing these essential tasks as well as a basis for discussing them with family members.

Shane, Dorlene V., and others. *Finances after 50: Financial Planning for the Rest of Your Life.* 1989. Harper, $19.95; Harper/Perennial, paper, $10.95.

Working under the auspices of the United Seniors Health Cooperative (a nonprofit consumer organization), Shane has developed various financial planning systems for those nearing or within retirement. Worksheets that can be photocopied for personal use define how to evaluate present income, housing, insurance, income tax, and investment situations. Thorough explanations include anecdotes of typical family situations with sample worksheets completely filled out. Besides aiding in future planning, these detailed instructions can help widowed individuals systematically analyze their financial situations. The combination of authentic situations and matter-of-fact directions works quite effectively even though the guide reads like a homework assignment with required materials and documents noted as each chapter opens. Instructions are also provided on estate planning and creating a personal financial plan. The nature and manner of purchase for common investments appear in an appendix, along with a glossary and recommended reading list.

Soled, Alex J. *The Essential Guide to Wills, Estates, Trusts, and Death Taxes.* 1987. An AARP Book published for the American Association of Retired Persons by Scott, Foresman; dist. by Little, Brown, $19.95; paper, $12.95.

Soled's guide explores the many ramifications of devising an effective will or trust. Using a question-and-answer format, he responds to a multitude of concerns that range from defining legal terms, such as testator and testatrix, to more complex considerations, such as the critical elements in estate planning. In conjunction with Theodore Hughes and David Klein's *A Family Guide to Wills, Funerals, and Probate,* this resource can help formulate a legal plan tailored to the individual's intentions, family, and assets. Death taxes are carefully explained in light of the 1986 Tax Reform Act. In the appendix, Soled provides charts and explanations of variations in rates, requirements, and compensations within each state. He presents a thoughtful summation of the requirements of these vital legal documents, geared toward the interests and probable needs of older citizens. Directions for performing these essential tasks and discussing them with family members are supplied.

See also *No Lifetime Guarantee: Dealing with the Details of Death,* by Katie Maxwell (page 53).

Social Security and Medicare

Bernstein, Merton C., and Joan Brodshaug Bernstein. *Social Security: The System That Works.* 1988. Basic Books, $21.95.

As their subtitle indicates, the Bernsteins consider the Social Security system an effective program; not the dinosaur many others claim it to be. This is no blithe decree. They supply an extensive history and contemporary survey to support their judgment. Merton Bernstein was principal consultant to the National Commission on Social Security Reform, and his coauthor and wife is an experienced agency administrator. In Chapter 2 ("What Went Wrong and How It Was Fixed") they explain the reform of Social Security in the 1980s. The Bernsteins also point out that many new decisions are yet to be made. Their discussion of retirement age includes some background on how age sixty-five was established and thought-provoking comment on its universal validity, especially today. Similarly, in an extensive look at private pension plans, the authors point out possible pitfalls and advantages. Conversational fodder abounds in the issues they raise and the solutions they suggest. Although primarily a conceptual book, it is written with such candor that both current and potential users of Social Security and Medicare will reach for it as a resource.

Rubin, Leona G. *Your 1989/1990 Guide to Social Security Benefits.* 1989. Facts on File, $18.95; paper, $9.95.

Rubin answers questions about Social Security in a clear, concise manner in this regularly updated book. It starts with the basics—what is Social Security, how do I obtain a card, how do I collect payment—and then explains retirement, disability, and survivors' benefits. Eligibility for Supplemental Security Income (established in 1974 for the aged, blind, and disabled) is spelled out and carefully distinguished from Social Security. Extensive coverage of Medicare is also provided. Each chapter details specific issues, then follows up with a question-and-answer section that further clarifies the information and allows coverage of specialized concerns. This format, plus an index conveniently printed in larger type, results in a physically convenient as well as informative book.

See also *Born to Pay: The New Politics of Aging in America,* by Phillip Longman (page 7).

Chapter 8

Biographies and Memoirs

"All my life I listened while people talked about growing old," says Leroy Daniels, the hundred-year-old horsetrader whose memoirs are included here. "I know this [aging] is a thing people fear, but I still don't know what it is. I felt the same at eighty, ninety, a hundred, as I did when I was twenty, only I have a lot more experience behind me now."

His experiences and those of other everyday people are included in this chapter along with stories of well-known writers, artists, politicians, and movie stars. These biographies and memoirs can be read for entertainment, insight, and a refresher course in the past century; those who are profiled have more than longevity to recommend them. Liz Carpenter, former aide to President Lyndon Johnson, mentions that she has lived almost a third as long as this country. Her adventures in the White House will entrance readers; yet even more relevant are her keen reactions to widowhood. Rare insight into the feelings of men as sons can be found in the memoirs of Philip Kunhardt and M. R. Montgomery, who alternately demonstrate how relationships with their fathers still affect them. The critical issues of aging are part of these lives. Biography as a genre is read for many reasons—from love of gossip to cultural enlightenment. These biographies can also open up family discussion and help reconcile emotions.

Calisher, Hortense. *Kissing Cousins: A Memory.* 1988. Weidenfeld & Nicholson, $14.95.

Calisher, a splendid novelist and story writer, looks deeply into her own complicated Jewish and Southern roots in this fine sample of memoir-writing. She sings the praises of her cousin Katie who has served as surrogate mother, confidante, and friend. After all, as Calisher explains, when you are in your eighties there are few people left who can still "quell an untidy thought with a withering glare." Katie still has this effect on her younger cousin. Similarly, there are few like Calisher who can hone the random impressions of childhood with meaningful recollections and astute judgments on kin and "kissing cousins"—defined "as members of the family in every respect except blood." She recalls her cousin's comforting presence in "that long ago family room across which Southern locutions had whizzed like those tiny, bunched firecrackers." Such a ritual is found again in a community of seniors to which Katie has retired. Calisher is visiting and once again, "from across the room Katie glinted at me." Finally, Calisher asks her cousin questions she has never raised. She evokes jagged realisms: her own mother's troubles, her uncle's pastimes, and her beloved cousin's private sorrows. These merge to create a more complete perception of fondly recollected, eccentric family life in this luminescent memoir.

Caray, Harry, with Bob Verdi. *Holy Cow!* 1988. Villard Books, div. of Random House, $17.95.

"Holy Cow!" is the trademark of Chicago Cubs announcer Harry Caray. His autobiography, written with the help of Bob Verdi, sportswriter for the *Chicago Tribune*, possesses just that tone of exuberance. Caray, an orphan raised by an aunt in St. Louis, was a diehard fan of the St. Louis Cardinals since age eight. He talked his way into a radio broadcasting job at twenty-five and stayed with his home team for twenty-five years when suddenly his contract was not renewed. That was a blessing for Chicago. After one year in Oakland, Caray came back to the Midwest and worked for the Chicago White Sox for eleven years before joining the Cubs. Caray talks baseball all through his book with the same sheer pleasure he conveys from the broadcaster's booth. In the opening pages Caray tells about the stroke he suffered in 1987 while playing cards. He says, "I felt no pain . . . did not lose consciousness . . . and was up about five hundred dollars." Paralysis on his right side and incoherent speech were the lingering effects. Caray tells how he worked to overcome these problems, especially his speech difficulties, by watching televised ball games, turning down the sound, and practicing the calls. Within months, Caray returned triumphantly to Wrigley Stadium. He has become a national figure, partly from the wide broadcasting range (including cable) of his local station, but primarily through his own inimitable personality, which has had a special impact upon America's favorite game.

Carpenter, Liz. *Getting Better All the Time*. 1987. Simon & Schuster, $17.95; Pocket, paper, $4.95; G. K. Hall Large Print Books, $21.95.

Carpenter's natural vivacity infuses her book on aging Texas style. In the opening pages she says, "Today I am sixty-five . . . I'm a third as old as our country." She is also a literary whirlwind that carries her readers right into the Texas of her foremothers and fathers, the Washington presidential scene from Roosevelt through Carter, and her retirement as a reflective nature lover, party-giver, and political organizer. Most famous as press secretary to Lady Bird Johnson and aide to President Johnson, Carpenter began her career as a reporter at Eleanor Roosevelt's first press conference. There are photographs of Carpenter with her children, U.S. presidents, and others of note (such as Queen Elizabeth) throughout this autobiography. There is an emphasis on family ties; Carpenter repeatedly quotes her mother, her older brother, and her grandson. In sentimental reflections on marriage and widowhood, Carpenter tells of the "enveloping sadness" following her husband's death in 1974 and her efforts to overcome bereavement. They had built a news bureau, raised two children, and shared thirty remarkable years. "I can't stand being a widow," Carpenter told a friend. "I flinch at the word." Here the book moves from memoir to personal adviser on facing widowhood and aging. Carpenter has a final word on the appropriate ceremony for her own death: "I want a good funeral. I want the church full. Hold it in a phone booth if everyone I know died first . . . I want good press . . . with some irreverent anecdotes about my life . . . I want friend and foe to know I had a whale of a good time walking about God's earth."

Daniels, Leroy Judson, as told to Helen Herrick. *Tales of an Old Horsetrader: The First Hundred Years*. 1987. Univ. of Iowa Pr., $24.95; paper, $9.95.

On a visit to Iowa in 1965, Herrick was entranced by the wonderful stories told by her eighty-three-year-old cousin, Daniels. Since age fourteen Daniels had been catching, gentling, and trading horses, raising sheep, herding cattle, and farming. He shares the romance of horses and laments the devaluation of this spirited, intelligent animal into a wealthy person's status symbol. He even mentions a meeting with Henry Ford in the Chicago stockyards (where he expressed disbelief in Ford's ambitions). Daniels' seemingly endless tales of catching wild horses, making wily—yet honest—deals, and transporting vast numbers of animals offer a rich legacy certain to arouse memories or educate a younger reader about the reality of a hard day's work. In his nineties Daniels made a new start; he opted to "go back to Iowa and feed a few more sheep and grow another garden." This was long after his son had retired from farming.

Horses were not the only romance in Daniels' life. He was married for fifty years. After the death of his first wife, a letter of consolation from an old friend led to his second marriage. When Daniels visited this former girlfriend, he recalls, "We still looked good to each other." He describes their marriage in a lyrical fashion: "The world was a more perfect place than it had ever been before for both of us." He is just as frank and moving about the emptiness he felt when she died. He mentions the shocked reactions of some people to his third marriage—"just thirteen days before my ninety-third birthday": "I guess they just don't understand how it is for two elderly people who are used to doing what people do—work, travel, and all that—and suddenly, it seems, finding themselves doing less and less, and then strokes or some other curse falls and they are left high and dry, like a seagull on a post." When Herrick finished compiling and editing these memoirs, Daniels was "still here to enjoy it." This book has all the adventure of a wild west show (as a child he also met Buffalo Bill) and a great deal of substance for reading again and again.

Gingold, Hermione, with Anne Clements Eyre. *How to Grow Old Disgracefully: My Life*. 1988. St. Martin's, $16.95.

When Gingold finished her autobiography, shortly before her death in 1987, she asked her friend Lady Eyre to "tidy up" her manuscript. Clearly the tidying up was purely mechanical for the book is filled with Gingold's voice. Bawdy tales and scandalous recollections outweigh serious thought. Gingold relives her days on stage, poring over the revues, plays, and other performances, citing her favorite lines, lovers, and costars. There were few of the latter, for Gingold hated to share the limelight, which she readily admits. With uncharacteristic tact, the eighty-one-year-old Gingold refers to her last, quite youthful lover simply as Little Big Boy. She reveals that "his mother would not like his name mentioned." This amusing memoir of a woman who played croquet with General Patton and strolled with Maurice Chevalier in the film *Gigi* is delightful and particularly intriguing for those who recall her stage performances.

Heard, Regie, and Bonnie Langenhahn. *Regie's Love: A Daughter of a Former Slave Recalls and Reflects*. 1987. McCormick & Schilling (P. O. Box 722, Menomonee Falls, WI 53051), paper, $7.95.

Heard, whose mother was born a slave in 1859, has been a teacher, cook, domestic servant, factory worker, entrepreneur, restaurant owner, and foster parent, to name some of her life's occupations. Coauthor Langenhahn met Heard as part of a writing-therapy program that Langenhahn developed at the Marian Catholic Home in Milwaukee, Wisconsin. Langenhahn's interest revived this grieving woman, whose husband had recently died. A friendship evolved from this sociological project, involving memoir writing for nursing home residents. The program was designed to "shatter the myth that age and institutional life suppress creativity, purpose, and strength." Heard's story has been expressed in a voice Langenhahn describes as "ours" since Heard disliked her accent as transcribed from her taped recollections. The narrative reads beautifully. Heard's enthusiasm for life fills the book, whether she is telling about childhood mischief in Washington, Arkansas, or the opening of her teashop in Milwaukee during the 1920s. A brief instruction on writing therapy prefaces this courageous black woman's fascinating personal journey. Both authors hope this memoir will stimulate similar autobiographical programs for the elderly elsewhere.

Joseph, Pleasant, and Harriet J. Ottenheimer. *Cousin Joe: Blues from New Orleans.* 1987. Univ. of Chicago Pr., $19.95.

Joseph, known to jazz fans throughout the world as Cousin Joe, told his life story to Ottenheimer. Over a twenty-year span (beginning in the 1960s) Ottenheimer, an anthropologist, taped and edited this life-story narrative. Their joint effort makes a stunning personal history that also fills in plenty of background on American music and society. Joseph spent part of his childhood, when he wasn't making mischief, dodging his father, "a mean man. . . . I was more afraid of my daddy than the Devil's afraid of holy water." Yet even more space is taken up with the hazards of Joseph's many love affairs. He says, "I don't know, I must have had magic or something. Women would just look at me and be ready to go." Then there's the music. The struggling jazz guitarist and blues singer's career went from ukulele performances at the shoe shop through bands, solo gigs, and street corner performances. Joseph mentions his work with many other jazz and blues greats, including Muddy Waters, Dizzy Gillespie, and Ella Fitzgerald—and is not shy about sharing their high opinion of him. Racism in the United States is dramatized when the authors contrast the story of Joseph being greeted by a motorcade in Cuba—shortly after he was forbidden to drink from a public water fountain by a Florida policeman. Financial stability did not arrive until the 1970s when he began playing regularly in Europe. By then he was named by the French "one of the four greatest blues singers in the United States."

Kunhardt, Philip. *My Father's House.* 1970. Random, O.P.

After a heart attack in 1963, the author's father died at age sixty-two. Four years later at forty-eight, Kunhardt suffered a serious heart attack. His own illness gave him the impetus to reflect upon his life as a son and as a parent. The father of five children, aged three to seventeen when he wrote this memoir, Kunhardt returned home from the hospital grateful for their affection and feeling openly sentimental about the mantle of fatherhood that he wears. In much of this book, he celebrates his own father, noting the man's flaws and recognizing that his absences from home due to business probably heightened the sense of excitement when he was there to throw a football, pitch a tent, or take a hike. The author shares the zest of family holidays, everyday life, and male family rituals, such as camping trips. After Kunhardt's own death scare, many thoughts surfaced about his grief for his father. He recalls, "my father spent the last year of his life fighting mightily to keep alive . . . crippled from a leg operation . . . [and beset with] trouble and pain from deadly uremic poisoning." Kunhardt's youthful memories and somber recollections of his father's last days reveal the forceful character of this remarkable and cherished man. Though intriguing in itself, Kunhardt's story may also serve as a springboard for similar reflections.

L'Engle, Madeleine. *Two-Part Invention: The Story of a Marriage.* 1988. Farrar, $17.95.

L'Engle, widely known for her children's books, celebrates her years of marriage to Hugh Franklin. A stage, film, and television actor, Franklin played Dr. Tyler in the soap opera "All My Children" for years. In Part I of her memoir, she recalls their courtship. Both were in theater and traveled, when there was work, with touring companies that could barely sustain these young actors. Their romantic adventures resemble a scene from modern daytime drama. Rather than a sequential memoir, the second half of the book is a neatly balanced record of their married life and recent difficulties. L'Engle alternates recollections of their forty-year marriage with a moving description of her husband's final illness from cancer. Fans of L'Engle's many books will want to read of her life; and those who have suffered through a loved one's severe illness will be heartened by her simple expressions of faith and affection.

Montgomery, M. R. *Saying Goodbye: A Memoir for Two Fathers.* 1989.
Knopf. $18.95.

Montgomery has written this memoir to say goodbye to his
father. It becomes readily apparent that the author had never spoken this intensely with his parent while he was alive. The emotional distance between Montgomery and his father comes across
from the beginning when he describes his dad in terms of the geol-
ogy, natural history, and politics that shaped his father's life. His
father worked as a civil engineer to help build the world's largest
earth-filled dam in Montana during the Depression and managed
U.S. Navy construction projects overseas throughout the Second
World War. As Montgomery affectionately, even reverently, discusses his Japanese father-in-law, the rift with his father becomes
obvious; it began in childhood due to wartime separation or clashing personalities and continued with his father's refusal to accept
Montgomery's Japanese wife. Comparing these two fathers, particularly during the war, is interesting, but the changing tone of this
narrative speaks volumes about the turmoil of that first father-son
relationship. The juxtaposition of his Japanese father-in-law,
whose medical career was halted by bigotry and wartime bureaucracy, and his technology-oriented parent presents a fascinating
microcosm of American history in the mid-twentieth century.

Pepper, Claude D., and Hays Gorey. *Pepper: Eyewitness to a Century.*
1987. Harcourt, $19.95.

In this lively self-portrait, Pepper pores over events of the
past century, citing the wonders and tribulations he has witnessed
without neglecting to describe his own contributions. Most widely
known as the octogenarian congressman involved in maintaining
the rights of the elderly, Pepper was born in rural Alabama in
September 1900 and was serving in Congress when he died in
1989. After holding an assortment of jobs from hat blocker to high
school teacher, this "former cotton picker and plowboy" attended
Harvard on a grant earned through his World War I military service. His verve and self-confidence (bordering on self-righteousness)
permeate these recollections of his legal and political careers. Considerable anger runs through his report on the McCarthyist tactics
that ended his early position as a U.S. senator, and a matching
pride shines forth in the telling of his comeback in the House of
Representatives later in life. If at times the memoirs sound like a
campaign speech, Pepper is doing what he knows best. Stories of
hobnobbing with presidents are balanced by expressions of outrage

at the ostracism practiced by former friends and political cohorts when he was out of office. Pepper's example, as a dedicated man working into his eighties, has done as much good for the image of the elderly as his political reforms achieved toward ensuring their financial and personal independence.

Sarton, May. *After the Stroke: A Journal.* 1988. Norton, $16.95.

Sarton is a multifaceted writer of fiction, poetry, and biography. Her journals provide not only a window into her life but thoughtful reflections on growing older as well. In her last journal, *At Seventy* (Norton, 1987), Sarton wrote, "My life at the moment is a little like a game of solitaire that is coming out. . . . The long hard work is bearing fruit. . . . I feel happy and at peace." That serenity was shattered by a stroke. In many pages of this new journal, Sarton reports on her fury and pain as she tries to recover physically. Worst of all, Sarton reports, "I feel so deprived of my self being unable to write." When she is at last able to cook again, to welcome guests, to appreciate the lively spirit of her cat, to relish her garden, and to write of these and other vital matters in her journal— the reader shares her joy of recovery. Anyone who has been seriously ill will know the strength even the smallest notations in this journal have required. They will also thoroughly understand her anguished rage with her weakness and the ineptitude of hospital staff when it occurs. When Sarton's professional life is resurrected in talks, tours, and writing poetry, this journal, like her many others, provides a piquant immersion in the life of a graceful, astute writer and a gentle, vibrant woman.

Tiede, Tom. *American Tapestry: Eyewitness Accounts of the Twentieth Century.* 1988. Pharos; dist. by Ballantine, $19.95.

Tiede has sought out men and women who were born near the turn of the century, solicited their recollections, and woven their memories into a topical survey of the twentieth century. Among his interviewees are soldiers, senators, crooks, farmers, ministers, entertainers, and activists—most with at least a modicum of fame attached to their names. An ex-vaudeville star chats about the temptations to which he succumbed; Margaret Chase Smith recalls her work in Congress; a witness from the Scopes trial offers his memories and opinions; and Maggie Kuhn talks about the founding of the Gray Panthers. Tiede adds corrections and criticism along with facts and figures to round out these neatly edited interviews (although some of his own research may at times merit corrections or criticism). These memoirs provide an intensely personal journey through the first eight decades of this century and an astute introduction to some of its liveliest characters.

Truitt, Anne. *Turn: The Journal of an Artist.* 1986. Penguin, paper, $6.95.

Truitt illuminates the process of coming "face to face with aging." As an artist and sculptor who has always worked on large projects, a grandmother who pursued toddling grandchildren, and a single woman who has led an independent life, Truitt was astonished by the physical toll of growing older. In these journal entries, she writes of this universal experience in spare, beautiful prose, using exact images. Truitt faces the death of her former husband, her daughter's divorce, a legal confrontation over inequities in her university salary, a tumultuous European vacation, and a taxing nine-month stint as acting director at Yadoo, the artists' community. As she records this rich variety of experiences and blends her own perceptions about change into them, Truitt offers challenges and lessons to others. Among her perceptions: "Tact is a subtle form of affection useful to the parents of married children." She finds that one of the compensations of aging is the requisite slower pace that "is as if I were tuning in to a deeper, slower resonance in music I have been listening to all my life without realizing that this profundity underlay more lively tunes." Truitt's realization is not a smooth, easy matter. "My turn toward aging began when I was fifty-nine and confounded me. . . . It seemed as if one day I was as strong as I had been all my adult life and the next found me stuck in a balky vehicle." Dismayed by her diminishing strength, she is equally frustrated by her inability to solve the problems of her grown children. However, she learns that her new sculptures can benefit from her lighter approach and that her new vision of her children as adults and her observations of their problem-solving are as gratifying as holding their hands when they were young and in need. Truitt's pensive memoir will captivate all those who scan its pages.

Warren, Robert Penn. *Portrait of a Father.* 1988. Univ. Pr. of Kentucky, $12.00.

Warren, the noted American poet, reflects upon his father's life and death in this remarkable elegiac essay. As his book opens, Warren states, "My father, as the years since his death pass, becomes to me more and more a man of mystery." Warren ponders the private sense of discipline that kept details of this man's personal history so obscure. Warren displays clues, as if they were archaeological findings that can bare hidden aspects of this admirable man. But Warren does not work with a pick or shovel; his technique is as restrained as those scientists who laboriously sift sand, pull out a tiny artifact, and treasure it. Warren's quest, and his lack of fury over not having every question consummately answered, provides an important lesson in this era of ancestor-searching that demands ferreting out every minute fact of family history. Gentle considerations, bemused speculations, and quiet, wondering grief are the qualities that make this portrait of a father so potent. This essay concludes with Warren's biographical poem, "Mortmain," written in response to his father's death.

Yeager, Chuck, and Charles Leerhsen. *Press On! Further Adventures in the Good Life.* 1988. Bantam, $17.95.

Yeager, the Air Force pilot who first flew faster than the speed of sound, shares some of his private pleasures and his own definition of the good life. However, this is not a reference to high living or extravagant tastes, for one of his most cherished times is backpacking in the Sierra Mountains far from other people. He also wrote *Yeager: An Autobiography* with Leo Janos in 1985 about his military exploits. In this memoir, he talks about his personal life and his "Hero Business." What else can he call the endless requests for speaking engagements, public appearances, television ads, and autographs? That business is ably run, according to this account, by Yeager's wife Glennis who knows exactly when to volunteer, whom to turn down, and which group to charge extraordinary fees. She personally reports on that aspect of their life. Her comments are only part of the intentional interruptions of the story. Old friends and family members comment on Yeager's life, work, and retirement; their stories broaden Yeager's modest description of his hunting, fishing, and flying days.

Chapter 9

Humor and Reflections

Comic recollections, semi-sweet humor, and witty advice can be found in these selections. Dr. Seuss writes to his geriatric peers in *You're Only Old Once* about coping with the medical merry-go-round. Milton Berle relives roasts at the Friar's Club since, it seems, the invention of fire. Evelyn Abrahams gives grandmother appreciation lessons. And Ralph Schoenstein shares his explorations of adult housing. These books will appeal to varying tastes in humor and yet reveal some truths about growing old.

Abrahams, Evelyn. *Mum's the Word: The Wit and Wisdom of a Semi-Sweet Grandmother.* 1985. Price Stern Sloan, $14.95.

Abrahams serves up advice about grandmotherhood with vigor and wit as she dispenses with the stereotype of grandma as an elderly woman with an ample bosom, spectacles, pleasant wrinkles, and so on. Such mythical grandmothers may exist, but Abrahams' collected comments from genuine grandmothers convincingly argue against this standard notion. Abrahams also outlines the dangers of the "Grandmother Trap"—a situation where an overzealous grandmother can make herself indispensable (and thoroughly exhausted). Another issue thoughtfully and humorously considered is that of "the other grandmother." The rivalry between such caring women could startle any pro football fan. These descriptions of competitive grandmothers, the debate over whether grandmothers are destined to babysit, and the value of letter-writing and gift-appreciation fill this book with warm and critical perceptions. This valuable analysis, actually a personalizing of the popular role played by mothers of children who have children, provides a lesson for the children and the mothers (even for the grandchildren if they are old enough to read this). After all, adult children must realize that their mothers have individual interests and abilities. At the same time, many women who desire to be an intimate part of their children's families are left to the good will of the local "Golden Age Center." The message here could easily be: grandmothers are people too—valuable individuals who should neither be forgotten nor overused.

Berle, Milton. *B. S. I Love You: Sixty Funny Years with the Famous and the Infamous.* 1988. McGraw-Hill, $17.95; paper, $7.95.

Berle's memoir is a history of the "world-famous Friars club . . . a fraternal organization with a mother branch in New York and a lusty offspring in Beverly Hills, California." He tells a bit of his own story first—"his inevitable march to the Friars"—truly inevitable for he had a strong-willed mother devoted to getting Miltie on stage and keeping him there. He first faced the Friars Round Table of show business professionals in 1920 (at age twelve), but his story goes back to its conception in 1907. The book is sprinkled with Berle's and everyone else's jokes, with at least one wisecrack or revealing anecdote between every serious sentence in the book. The reader will learn the lines and backstage adventures of George Raft, Jackie Coogan, Will Rogers, Sophie Tucker, George Jessel, Al Jolson, Red Skelton, Jimmy Durante, Harpo Marx, and dozens of other stars. Along with the jokes, slips, mishaps, and accomplishments of club members, Berle tells about his own life including references to his bypass surgery. More than a few jabs are aimed at the elder statesman of comedy, George Burns, who wrote a foreword for this book joking, "Milton Berle's head is a storehouse of show business details. Why not? There's nothing else in there." There is certainly much material here for those who enjoy risqué jokes, vaudeville reminiscences, and chats with some of America's funniest entertainers.

Brown, David. *Brown's Guide to Growing Gray.* 1987. Delacorte, $12.95.

This undersized advice/humor volume of quotations has been put together by the coproducer of such popular movies as *Cocoon* and *Jaws*. Brown obviously feels his own life experience is readily adaptable for all those growing gray. He proclaims: "The American dream of early retirement has turned out to be a nightmare," and "Don't marry for companionship. Friendship and companionship are more likely to be based upon sex than common interests." As this filmmaker lectures on divorce, marriage, and lovers, he frequently quotes his wife, Helen Gurley Brown, the editor of *Cosmopolitan*. While the sustenance of sex and work seems to be his major goal as he ages, Brown also shares private insights into other aspects of life. Advice on coping with failing physique, poor memory, and depression is balanced by encouraging words on the benefits of friendship and travel. It's a silly book, but Brown writes with a zest that may deliver a bit of oomph to his peers.

Dight, Janet. *Do Your Parents Drive You Crazy? A Survival Guide for Adult Children.* 1987. Prentice-Hall, $15.95.

   Dight, inspired by her credentials as an adult offspring of loving parents who smother her when she visits and induce guilt when she does not, shares her own recipes for getting along with parents. Dight describes many outrageous character types of fathers and mothers, including the worrier, the escapist, the scorekeeper, the pusher, the recruiter, the tyrant, and the insulter. For each type Dight suggests ways that adult offspring should respond—complete with possible forms of dialogue, sample scenarios, and encouragement to simply walk out. At first it appears that only the parents require personality transplants, never their grown offspring; then the author mentions that many parents treat their adult children like kids because they act that way. Dight also discusses other important issues such as borrowing money, visits, holiday planning, and raising the grandchildren. Considered as humor, her pop psychology makes a fine counterpoint to Evelyn Abrahams' book, *Mum's the Word* (page 97), and several titles in Chapter 2 on family relations. Dight's book overflows with thought-provoking characterizations and suggestions for promoting family harmony—or at least a cease-fire.

Schoenstein, Ralph. *Every Day Is SUNDAY.* 1986. Little, Brown, O.P.

   Schoenstein evaluated a few senior housing communities and reports his findings in a tongue-in-cheek fashion. When he first refers to exclusive senior housing as "sunny internment," the reader can be forewarned of his mischievous nature and built-in prejudices. He toured residential communities in the East, Florida, Arizona, and California. With wry humor that mellows even his fiercest criticism, Schoenstein evaluates the individual virtues and drawbacks of each community. This interesting, first-hand perusal of retirement living has its somber and outrageous moments. Stories of his acclaim on the dance floor (as the only single, willing, and able male) are balanced by more serious thoughts. He is incredibly moved by the deterioration of a close friend, a former professor who has settled into a retirement village. He blames the nonstimulating environment for his friend's mental and physical lethargy. From the beginning Schoenstein has doubts about the whole concept of segregated living for senior citizens. Still, his humor may entertain those comfortably settled in their retirement condos or apartments and will definitely offer food for thought to those seriously considering such a change in lifestyle.

Seuss, Dr. *You're Only Old Once!* 1986. Random, $10.95.

Dr. Seuss let loose in a geriatric clinic is a sight to behold. This colorful picture book has the same size and appearance as his popular children's books like *The Cat in the Hat*, but this one was really designed for the author's peers (Seuss dedicates it "with affection to the Class of 1925"). As the story opens, a balding, mustachioed gent "who is simply not feeling his best" waits in a lobby of the "Golden Years Clinic on Century Square for Spleen Readjustment and Muffler Repair." He is led through a tangle of corridors and subjected to outrageous exams, including the "Eyesight and Solvency Test." There is even a "Diet-Devising Computerized Sniffer":

> on which you just simply lie down in repose
> and sniff at good food as it goes past your nose.
> And when that guy finds out
> what you like,
> you can bet it
> won't be on your diet.

The zany, colorful drawings show the poor patient stuck in outrageous contraptions that capture the awful absurdity of so many real medical tests. The odes to pill-taking and bill-paying are sure to strike an amusing, probably familiar note.

White, Betty. *Betty White in Person.* 1987. Doubleday, $16.95.

White, one of the stars of the popular television series, "The Golden Girls," offers sincere, often comic musings on a wide range of subjects. She explains the aimless nature of her book: "My memory has always been lousy. . . . That's why, whenever I have been asked to write my 'memoirs,' I pass. There is just no way I can fill in the blanks." White is quite unaffected and consistently amusing in these rambling reflections on aging, pets, marriage, Hollywood, hate and guilt, only children, widowhood, and memory lapses, to name only a few of her chosen topics. Most of the book is filled with cozy lessons learned from her attentive parents or during her years as a "working girl." In a particularly moving section she discusses caring for her mother during her final illness. Throughout her book,

White brings up references to her childhood, her late husband, Allen Ludden, and to the famous folk who make up her "super-friends"—such as Mary Tyler Moore and Burt Reynolds. Those seeking an autobiography or Hollywood gossip (except for affectionately comic anecdotes about the other golden girls) will not find it here. White's many fans will relish these selected insights and opinions, presented in a chatty essay format that is easy to pick up for a quick, cheery read.

Chapter 10

Poetry

"When I am an old lady I shall wear purple,
with a red hat which doesn't go . . .
I shall sit down on the pavement when I am tired . . .
And run my stick along the public railings
and make up for the sobriety of my youth . . ."

Jenny Joseph's poem, "Warning," carries a challenge and an irresistible promise (this poem is reprinted in Sandra Martz's anthology reviewed on page 105). Throughout this bibliography books have been chosen that celebrate old age without being unrealistic about its trials, pains, and confusions. The poets included here display a bracing reality while continuing to revel in the beauty of the ageless human spirit. It is exhilarating to participate in the romantic verse of Archibald MacLeish, the grieving phrases of Paul Mariani, and the refreshing country poems of Maxine Kumin. These poems about families, aging, and death are not morbid or placating verse, but unique thoughts by diverse writers. Although these works were chosen for their quality and relevant subject matter, not as bibliotherapy, they have the potential to brighten spirits, free suppressed emotions, and otherwise enhance readers' lives.

Atwood, Margaret. *Selected Poems II: Poems Selected and New, 1976–1986.* 1987. Houghton Mifflin, $16.95; paper $9.95.

Atwood is a wonderfully versatile author who writes criticism, stories, and novels as well as poetry. As in her fiction, her poetry carries an imaginative, poignant call for human justice on a personal and political level. A vigorous feminist, Atwood declares women's anguish in novel, breathtaking word patterns. Her form is more comfortably conventional and humorous than the radical structures of Adrienne Rich (reviewed on page 106). For this anthology, Atwood has culled favorite poems from her three previous collections and added seventeen new ones. All are from the mid-1970s and early 1980s. Her pieces are filled with stark images and sharp humor, such as this excerpt from "Five Poems for Grand-mothers":

> Goodbye, mother
> of my mother, old bone
> tunnel through which I came.

Among the new poems of the 1980s are several with titles that begin "Aging Female Poet . . . " (Sits on the Balcony, Does Laundry, Reads Little Magazines). The changing details of her own maturation are placed in a context of universal significance and aptly captured in these poems with plain-spoken titles.

Kumin, Maxine. *Our Ground Time Here Will Be Brief.* 1982. Penguin, paper, $8.95.

Kumin's poems, rooted as they are in her life on a small New England horse farm, possess a comfortable solidity. She writes of uncles, hornflies, harvests, her own inklings of death, and a neighbor who "has outlasted Stalin, Roosevelt, and Churchill." This volume contains poems selected from Kumin's six earlier collections and several new pieces. Her graceful ruminations on adult offspring, the prospect of old age, and the death of friends and relatives are presented here in nimble, subtle lines of thought. For example, she writes about a visit with her married daughter:

> Now that the children have changed
> into exacting adults. . . .
>   I visit,
> playing a walk-on part with my excursion ticket
> that does not prevent my caring with secret frenzy
> about this woman, this child no longer a child.

Her passion for the land is nearly as strong as for her children. The growth of crops and livestock and their wintering seasons are a natural counterpart to Kumin's poetic reminiscences of friends and relatives who have also moved through nature's cycles. The constant natural and spiritual references blend with Kumin's graceful humor and banish morbidity from her poems.

MacLeish, Archibald. *Collected Poems, 1917–1982.* 1985. Houghton Mifflin, $19.95; paper, $12.95.

MacLeish, who died in 1982, had nearly a century to gather reflections for his poetry (and prose and drama). He was Librarian of Congress, a Pulitzer Prize winner, presidential adviser, and, in a sense, a national literary arbiter. This collection of 300 poems shows how much his writing is a blend of the political and the personal. The reader will be fascinated to realize how much he used American history to form his conventional verse, from his earliest publications to his last writings (assembled for publication by MacLeish's literary executor, Richard B. McAdoo). Other than providing a foreword to these miscellaneous works McAdoo includes no explanatory or critical remarks; yet he has added poems that MacLeish felt too personal to publish during his lifetime. His poems reveal many amusing, sensitive thoughts on growing old. What a joy it is to juxtapose the metaphorical passion in "The Happy Marriage" from 1924 against the knowing passion of "The Old Gray Couple." Here is a passage from the later poem:

> He: Fifty years ago we drew each other,
>   magnetized needle toward the longing north.
>   It was your naked presence that so moved me
>   It was your absolute presence that was love.
> She: Ah, was!
> He: And now, years older, we begin to see
>   absence not presence: what the world would be
>   without your footstep in the world—the garden
>   empty of radiance where you are.
>
> She: And that's your reason?—that old lovers see
>   their love because they know what its loss will be? . . .
> He: Ours is the late, last wisdom of the afternoon.
>   We know that love, like light, grows dearer toward the
>   dark.

Mariani, Paul. *Prime Mover.* 1985. Grove, $22.50; paper, $7.95.

Mariani's poems are as penetrating as Harold Kushner's prose and often ponder the same timeless question, "Why do bad things happen to good people?" (Kushner's book with this title is reviewed on page 46). This question is also asked in Mariani's final poem, "Then Sings My Soul":

> Who can tell a man's real pain
> —or a woman's either—when they learn
> the news at last that they must die?

POETRY 105

The poem turns into the story of Lenny, "a Spaniard of great dignity" with an aged mother and a family to support, who learns he is dying. The poem then becomes a prayer as Mariani says:

> "Lord, listen to the sound of my voice
> Grant Lenny health and long life. Or, . . .
> Grant me too the courage
> to face death when it shall notice me,
> when I shall still not understand why
> there is so much sorrow in the world."

Mariani's writing reveals a beautiful blend of classical and modern influences with theological and cultural references settled amid simple truths. He writes about war, ailing parents, death and dying. His scene of a teenage son frightened by his grandfather's cancer is dynamic. The poet's sensitive words do not exploit these common fears. Mariani's Catholic influence, as seen in his title poem about Geertgen's "small painting of Madonna and Child," helps to illumine his words on death. While they necessarily carry sadness, the poems also bear an echo of bliss.

Martz, Sandra, ed. *When I Am Old I Shall Wear Purple: An Anthology of Short Stories and Poetry.* 1987. Papier-Mâché Pr. (34 Malaga Place East, Manhattan Beach, CA 90266), paper, $10.00.

Martz, the editor and publisher of this stirring collection of stories, poetry, and photographs, selected her title from a poem by Jenny Joseph entitled, "Warning" (quoted in the introduction to this section). Emotional contemplations and biting images, accompanied by sharply accurate black-and-white portraits of aging women, fill the pages of this anthology. In sixty quite varied short stories and poems, the authors make clear the individuality of old women. The feelings of an "athlete growing old," a woman coming to understand why her widowed mother "dipped snuff," and a lesbian family are shared along with more traditional sentiments. These writers share the reality of aging and being old—the solitude, the lack of sex, the physical changes, and the satisfaction of wisdom gleaned even when unacknowledged. The intimacy, humor, and unpolished nature of these short stories and poems should touch people old and young. The appended notes on the contributors can lead readers to further works by these generally unknown authors.

Masterson, Dan. *Those Who Trespass.* 1985. Univ. of Arkansas Pr., $9.95; paper, $5.95.

In some of these poems Masterson speaks with the voice of the disabled and the dying, but mostly he speaks as a bereft son whose father has died and whose mother has become mentally and physically incapacitated. In "Opening Doors" the poet writes:

> He was staring at the red-ribbed chair
> where his father should be . . .
> He lay back and let it come, all . . . the talks,
> with his father, the papers that would take over
> at his death: what would become of Mother,
> the house, the land.

In "Night Sky" he writes about a son overwhelmed with the burden of visiting his mother in a nursing home.

> O, Father,
> there on the tallest star,
> I promised you too much
> for my own good. I cannot go
> daily to your wife.
> . . . my own impending age
> closes in like winter chill
> about my legs.

Masterson's collection closes with the title poem, a lengthy recording of an unusual legacy. A young man returns to his parents' former home, and using black paint he creates a giant rosary out of the rock garden. Prayers are said and memories restored during this wearying, penitential act of vandalism. The stories told in these poems are filled with realism and heartfelt drama.

Rich, Adrienne. *Your Native Land, Your Life.* 1986. Norton, $14.95; paper $6.95.

Rich is a talented poet whose powerful language speaks for the downtrodden in society. While this is not specifically a book of poems on aging, its relevance is twofold. First, there is a strong autobiographical section that illuminates the poet as a grown woman wrestling, through poetry, with oppressive paternal influences that still haunt her life. At one point she asks:

> how can I show you what I'm barely
> coming into possession of, invisible luggage
> of more than fifty years, looking at first
> glance like everyone else's, turning up
> at the airport carousel

Later in this slim volume of poetry, a selection called "Contradictions: Tracking Poems" contains a particularly poignant vision of illness and hospitalization. Rich issues an angry, provocative comparison between human illness (and the bullying forces of those in control of one's health) and the plight of the earth and its people.

> remember: the body's pain and the pain on the streets
> are not the same   but you can learn . . .
> The problem is
> to connect, without hysteria, the pain
> of any one's body with the pain of the body's world . . .
> *They call this elective surgery*
> *but we have all died of this.*

These lines demonstrate the ferocity of Rich's feelings as she tries to create a sense of universe that will not be ignored. Rich is not a comfortable, pastoral poet. She is a feminist, a humanist who uses her significant skills to awaken readers.

See also *I Never Told Anybody: Poetry Writing in a Nursing Home,* by Kenneth Koch (page 67), and Robert Penn Warren's biographical poem "Mortmain" in his memoir, *Portrait of a Father* (page 95).

Chapter 11

Plays and Films

Plays

The following plays reflect concerns and attitudes on aging. There are somber portrayals such as *The Gin Game*, and comic ones like *The Sunshine Boys*. In one of Neil Simon's later plays (*Broadway Bound*), the grandfather's sage asides are poignant reminders of the correlation between wisdom and aging. As with film and books, this list cannot be all-inclusive, yet it may lead readers, performers, and playgoers down some new avenues. Many of these plays were made into films as well. If there is a wide appeal for both the play and the film, a description appears in both sections, with the cross-reference "See also films." Other plays are simply annotated "Also a film."

For those plays currently available as books, the date, publisher, and current price are noted. The plays are all available in script format from specialized publishers and distributors (listed in *Literary Market Place* and *Publishers, Distributors, and Wholesalers of the United States*). The two major houses are Samuel French, Inc., and Dramatists Play Service. Librarians may purchase a script and have it bound in hardcover; individuals interested in performing these plays can write and obtain information on copyrights and costs.

Broadway Bound. By Neil Simon. 1987. Random House, $11.95; NAL, paper, $6.95.

This finale to Simon's autobiographical trilogy, preceded by *Brighton Beach Memoirs* and *Biloxi Blues*, tells of the launching of Simon's career as a radio writer. He shares the stage with his grandfather, who is struggling to sustain his independent lifestyle, political principles, and his daughter's marriage. The grandfather is a pillar of family life and a source of humorous material for his loving grandsons. Also a film.

Da. By Hugh Leonard. 1978. Atheneum, paper, $4.95.

The Irish patriarch of the play's title is already dead as the story opens but he remains a powerful influence as his son ruminates on his father's life and relives scenes from it.

Driving Miss Daisy. By Alfred Uhry. 1988. Theatre Communication Group, $15.95; paper, $6.95.

This enchanting story covers a span of twenty-five years and looks at the relationship between Miss Daisy, a southern Jewish woman, and the black chauffeur hired by her son. Their growing mutual respect and affection are conveyed through simple dialogue and finely drawn incidents. Also a film.

The Duck Variations. By David Mamet.

As two elderly men sit on a park bench and observe nature, especially the ducks in a pond, they exchange observations about life, aging, and death.

The Gin Game. By D. L. Coburn.

In a bleak nursing home, a man and woman meet, begin a game of gin rummy, and share a revealing conversation about their lives and families. They querulously pursue a sorry but necessary friendship. Jessica Tandy and Hume Cronyn made this Pulitzer Prize-winning play a Broadway hit. Also a film.

I'm Not Rappaport. By Herb Gardner. 1988. Grove, $7.95.

Two octogenarians share a park bench and their clashing opinions on life. One is a black apartment superintendent and the other a lifelong radical.

La Cage aux Folles. By Jean Poiret.

This hilarious, gala musical is filled with song-and-dance scenes and bawdy humor replete with the pathos of aging (especially as felt by the show's star). It revolves around an intergenerational conflict set off by the upright young son of a nightclub owner who tries to hide his father's lifestyle from the rigid family of his fiancée. His concern is not only his parent's homosexuality but the fact that the gala chorus line is manned—literally—by men in female attire.

'Night Mother. By Marsha Norman. 1983. Hill & Wang, $6.95.

A young woman busily prepares her household and her mother for her death one evening as she plans to commit suicide.

The frank, funny, searing conversations between mother and daughter touch on many critical issues, especially the young woman's epilepsy and broken marriage. Also a film.

The Petition. By Brian Clark.

An elderly couple review their lifetime of political and personal differences and reflect upon how dissent has exerted a continual influence on their lives.

The Road to Mecca. By Athol Fugard. 1988. Theatre Communications Group, $14.95; paper, $6.95.

An independent, yet increasingly frail, widowed sculptor is seen as an anomaly in her small South African town. When a well-intentioned church leader tries to have her admitted to a retirement/nursing home, she fights for her private life and calls on a young woman friend from Cape Town to support her. Winner of New York Critic's Best Foreign Play in 1988.

Salonika. By Louise Page. 1983. Heinemann ed. paper, $4.95.

A retired English spinster and her mother stay at a Greek seaside resort where the issues of war, mother-daughter relationships, and indignities of old age are confronted. Also a film.

A Separate Peace. By Tom Stoppard.

In this play, which first appeared on television, an elderly man who wishes only for a peaceful, anonymous lifestyle, befuddles and distresses the staff of a nursing home.

The Shadow Box. By Michael Cristofer.

This play about three families awaiting the death of an irascible old woman is set in a hospital for the terminally ill. The Pulitzer prize– and Tony award–winning play is charged with realism and humor.

The Sunshine Boys. By Neil Simon.

A pair of vaudeville performers in their seventies are summoned out of retirement for a television special in this comic play. See also films.

Tribute. By Bernard Slade.

Jack Lemmon received a Tony award for his role as a terminally ill screen writer who seeks a reconciliation with his estranged wife and an adult son whom he has neglected. See also films.

Two Masters: A Play in Two Parts. By Frank Manley.

   In "The Rain of Terror" an elderly couple reflect upon their run-in with an escaped criminal. In the second part, "An Errand of Mercy," a stroke victim in a nursing home is visited by two women friends.

The Whales of August. By David Berry.

   Two aging sisters of clashing temperaments are both saddened by the realization that they will soon lose their independence. See also films.

Whose Life Is It Anyway? By Brian Clark. Avon, paper, $2.95.

   A youthful sculptor, paralyzed in an auto accident, insists on his right to die. Clark's play dramatizes a stunning pursuit of this difficult civil and moral controversy. See also films.

   See also *New Plays for Mature Actors,* ed. by Bonnie L. Vorenberg (page 67).

Feature Films

The following videos were selected as samples of recent (since 1970) feature films that either talk directly about aging or demonstrate more subtly the fact that much of life remains to be experienced. Comedies, Westerns, romances, dramas, and science fiction are included. The stories are not necessarily about aging, but most feature older characters or significant concerns (such as terminal illness or parent and grown child relationships). The list is far from exhaustive, but the themes, actors, and links to the original books and plays will offer new leads for entertainment. For the convenience of home viewing, only films currently available in video format are cited (along with the current distribution company). Prices fluctuate to such a degree that listing them would not be helpful; distributors remain the best source for this information, and their telephone numbers and addresses can be found in the annual *AV Marketplace* (Bowker) or *The Video Source Book* (Gale, annual).

The Autobiography of Miss Jane Pittman. 1973. 110 min. Prism. Directed by John Katz.

   In 1962 a valiant black woman, 110-year-old Jane Pittman, played by Cicely Tyson, imparts a personal history of the past century from the Civil War to Civil Rights. Made for television, this drama won nine Emmy awards.

Cocoon. 1985. 117 min. CBS. Directed by Ron Howard.

　　Hume Cronyn, Don Ameche, and Wilfred Brimley play seniors who are physically rejuvenated by swimming in a pool that has been used to hide alien life forms (cocoons). The blend of sci-fi with the truisms of aging makes a remarkable movie based upon a novel by David Saperstein. A sequel, *Cocoon II*, has been released in video format.

The Dresser. 1983. 118 min. RCA. Directed by Peter Yates.

　　An aging Shakespearean actor known only as Sir, played by Albert Finney, is alternately coddled and vilified by his dresser and servant (Tom Courtenay) as he eloquently spouts Shakespeare and misses his calls. Based on the play by Ronald Harwood.

Educating Rita. 1983. 110 min. RCA. Directed by Lewis Gilbert.

　　A British college professor (Michael Caine) finds his life illumined by a brash, young, cockney woman (Julie Walters) whose search for education excites his love of literature and life. Originally a play by Willie Russell.

The First Deadly Sin. 1980. 112 min. Warner. Directed by Brian Hutton.

　　A New York cop approaching retirement must battle the bureaucracy to sustain his search for a maniac killer; meanwhile his wife lies dying of an undiagnosed illness. Based upon the novel by Laurence Saunders.

Going in Style. 1979. 96 min. Warner. Directed by Martin Brest.

　　Starring George Burns, Art Carney, and Lee Strasberg, this movie about three retirees in Queens who, out of boredom, plan and pull off a stick-up of a New York City bank has its contemplative and comic moments.

The Grey Fox. 1983. 92 min. MED. Directed by Philip Borsos.

　　Based on the life of Bill Miner, Canada's gentleman bandit, this beautifully filmed story stars Richard Farnsworth and Jackie Burroughs. Miner's venture into train stick-ups and romance following his release from prison makes a moving story.

Harry and Tonto. 1974. 115 min. CBS. Directed by Paul Mazursky.

In an Oscar-winning performance, Art Carney plays a widower who leaves the stifling environment of his son's suburban house to travel with his cat, Tonto, across the country. He tries out living with his other grown children and discovers that he likes traveling best.

The Karate Kid. 1984. 126 min. RCA. Directed by John G. Avildsen.

Noriyuki "Pat" Morita teaches karate to a fatherless, bullied teen (Ralph Macchio). The growing friendship between the old man and boy is also a very deliberate display of the talents and troubled past of this elderly Japanese-American.

Madame Rosa. France 1977; U.S. 1978. 105 min. Vestron. Directed by Moshe Mizrahi.

Simone Signoret plays Madame Rosa, an aging ex-prostitute who cares for the children of other women of the street. A special friendship evolves between her and a fourteen-year-old Arab boy in this touching French film dubbed in English. Based upon the novel by Emile Ajar—the pseudonym of Romain Gary.

The Mirror Crack'd. 1980. 105 min. Thorn. Directed by Guy Hamilton.

In this Agatha Christie mystery Jane Marple, played by Angela Lansbury, is laid up in her village cottage and must solve a murder for a visiting movie company. An all-star cast of suspects highlights this film.

Nothing in Common. 1986. 118 min. Tri-Star. Directed by Garry Marshall.

Jackie Gleason plays the irascible father of an egocentric advertising man (Tom Hanks) who reluctantly becomes caught up in his parents' lives when they separate. Plenty of intergenerational conflict and aging concerns are slipped in around a story that focuses mainly on the love life and career challenges of Hanks's character.

On Golden Pond. 1981. 109 min. CBS. Directed by Mark Rydell.

Henry Fonda and Katharine Hepburn play the Thayers, a couple married for forty-eight years. Fonda's character is nearly eighty and works through some trying, fruitful moments with his daughter (played by Jane Fonda) and her fiancé's teenage son. Also a play by Ernest Thompson who wrote the original novel and received an academy award for this screenplay.

Ran. 1985. 161 min. CBS/Fox. Directed by Akiro Kurosawa.

   In this Japanese film, based on *King Lear*, Tatsuya Nakadai plays a warlord whose attempts to divide his kingdom peacefully among his three sons is met with anguish and betrayal.

The Shootist. 1976. 99 min. Paramount. Directed by Don Siegel.

   In his last film, John Wayne plays a famous gunslinger dying of cancer who tries in vain to spend his final days anonymously in a boarding house, the owner of which is played by Lauren Bacall. Based upon the novel by Glendon Swarthout.

The Sunshine Boys. 1975. 111 min. MGM/UA. Directed by Herbert Ross.

   Walter Matthau and George Burns play cranky vaudeville performers in their seventies who have not spoken to one another for a decade. Their reunion for a television special is hilarious. Burns made an Oscar-winning comeback of his own (his previous film was released in 1939). Based on Neil Simon's play.

Terms of Endearment. 1983. 132 min. Paramount. Directed by James L. Brooks.

   This Oscar-winning film about a young woman facing terminal illness has as its backdrop a tumultuous mother-daughter relationship played out over thirty years and stars Debra Winger and Shirley MacLaine. Based on the novel by Larry McMurtry.

Tough Guys. 1986. 104 min. Disney. Directed by Jeff Kanew.

   Burt Lancaster and Kirk Douglas play infamous robbers who upon their release from prison are agog at the changes the decades have brought. They cannot conform and finally decide to prove their mettle by pulling off a daring train robbery.

Tribute. 1980. 123 min. Vestron. Directed by Bob Clark.

   Jack Lemmon plays a failed screenwriter dying of a rare blood disease who seeks reconciliation with his estranged wife and their adult son. Lemmon also played this role in the play written by Bernard Slade.

The Trip to Bountiful. 1985. 106 min. Embassy. Directed by Peter Masterson.

   In an Oscar-winning performance, Geraldine Page plays an old woman living with her controlling son and daughter-in-law. She finds the gumption to make a solitary, restorative journey to her home-town of Bountiful. Based on the play by Horton Foote.

The Whales of August. 1987. 90 min. Nelson. Directed by Lindsay Anderson.

In a scenically and emotionally beautiful movie, Lillian Gish and Bette Davis play two elderly, dissimilar sisters faced with the decision of giving up their independence as well as their family home on an island off the coast of Maine. Originally a play by David Berry.

Where's Poppa? 1970. 82 min. Key. Directed by Carl Reiner.

An elderly mother (Ruth Gordon) deemed senile hilariously fends off her youngest son's suitors and wreaks havoc in her other son's married life. A not exactly sensitive portrait of aging, but there are some dark comic scenes, especially the investigation of nursing homes. Based on the novel by Robert Klane.

White Mama. 1980. 105 min. MCA. Directed by Jackie Cooper.

Bette Davis plays an impoverished woman who eventually becomes a bag lady. Her attempts to stave off poverty by acting as foster mother to a black juvenile defender bring her lessons on street life and offer the teen new perceptions as well. Originally a made-for-television drama.

Whose Life Is It Anyway? 1981. 118 min. MGM. Directed by John Badham.

Richard Dreyfuss plays a young sculptor whose paralysis from an auto accident provokes him to insist that he has the right to die. Powerful, moving treatment of a critical issue. Based on the play by Brian Clark.

Community Interest and Educational Videos

Many issues about aging are uniquely suited to video. They do not deal solely with how-to's, such as Richard Simmons exercising with the Silver Foxes. Library video producers have done an excellent job producing educational, entertaining releases. Some of the most touching concern relations between grandparents and their progeny, like *The Electric Grandmother,* that can be enjoyed by audiences of all ages. Documentaries on travel, CPR, shoplifting, and home care are enlightening and helpful.

The resource consulted for most of these titles was *Video for Libraries* (ALA, 1988) with the permission of editors Sally Mason and James Scholtz. As explained in their introduction, "The titles suggested are a mixture of inexpensive 'home-use-only' tapes and the more expensive educational and informational tapes from educational producers. . . . Many of the educational and informational tapes are unique. They are made especially for the education and library market and contain material not available on low-cost video. The price is higher because the potential sales cannot compete with, say, an exercise tape or a feature film that has earned its money back at the box office. Most of these higher-priced tapes include public performance rights, meaning they can be used in library programs and with community groups."

A senior center or residence that cannot afford to purchase these videos can often arrange for a presentation or even borrow them from their library (or the state library film co-op). For direct purchase, distributors are cited after each title. Their addresses may be obtained from the current edition of *AV Marketplace,* published annually by Bowker.

Booklist, the review journal published by the American Library Association, is an ongoing evaluative source of recommended videos on all subjects, including aging, suitable for programming with seniors. Winners of the National Media Awards of the Retirement Research Foundation also include choice films and videos specifically on aging; a catalog is available from the foundation (1300 Higgins Rd., Suite 214, Park Ridge, IL 60068). One other nonevaluative reference for additional titles is *The Video Source Book* (now in its tenth edition), published by Gale.

A Better View of You. 1985. 18 min. New York Lighthouse, $50.

   Many older people suffer from a wide array of vision problems. This useful program discusses how to prevent, treat, and cope with them.

Aging in America: Dignity or Despair?—Aging and the Family. 1989. 162 min. Frank Beach, $150.

   A four-part teleconference moderated by Ted Koppel, who incisively questions experts on crises regarding aging, examines the effects of caring for older relations on families, and exposes the inadequate resources available for information and emotional support.

Aging in Soviet Georgia: A Toast to Sweet Old Age. 1987. 54 min. Filmakers Library, $325.

This search for the truth behind the rumors that Soviet Georgians live well past one hundred years old ends up looking at the life of one eighty-four-year-old woman, her family, and peers. This realistic study of everyday life in the Soviet Union is an excellent myth-shatterer in many ways. In an epilogue, the filmmakers, Maggie Kuhn (founder of the Gray Panthers), and a noted gerontologist debate about how aging is treated differently in the United States and the Soviet Union.

Armchair Fitness. 1984. 60 min. CC-M Productions, $39.95.

Betty Switkes enthusiastically leads a group of people through three aerobic workouts. All of the exercises are designed to be done from a sitting position, which makes them ideal for physically challenged people.

At Home with Home Care. 1985. 140 min. Billy Budd Films, $695.

A basic, no-frills guide for the home caregiver, including fourteen ten-minute segments. Subjects covered include emergencies, nutrition, grooming the patient, medication, moving the patient, and other essential information.

CPR: It's about Time. 1987. 25 min. American Heart Association, $150.

Unlike any other program on cardiopulmonary resuscitation, this fine production is designed to be used independently of classroom instruction. Viewers are urged to absorb what they can from its personal testimony and professional demonstrations of CPR techniques and to apply them in an emergency.

The Dream and the Triumph. 1986. 26 min. Beacon Films, $149.

In this film based on the story of Ernest Buckler, a young man is torn between pursuing his dream of becoming an engineer and returning to help his grandmother run the farm where he grew up.

Elderhostel. 1989. 10 min. Elderhostel (80 Boylston St., Suite 400, Boston, MA 02116), $10.

This is basically an advertisement for the university-linked program of entertaining education for seniors. A narrator explains the world of fun, companionship, and enlightenment available for any interested adult over sixty, while lively music plays and scenes are shown of seniors listening, conversing, hiking, and exploring. Foreign-language versions are also available.

The Electric Grandmother. 1982; released 1987. 49 min. LCA/New World Video, $19.95.

An excellent adaptation of Ray Bradbury's heart-warming short story, "I Sing the Body Electric," this program stars Maureen Stapleton as a mechanical grandmother who enters into a family and immediately wins the hearts of all the children save one.

The Gift of Life. 1985. 49 min. Carousel Film and Video, $435.

Through profiles of individuals of various ages awaiting organ transplants, this informative, eye-opening documentary humanizes organ-transplant surgery and raises questions concerning its future implications and effects on patients, their families, and medicine in general.

Grandma Didn't Wave Back. 1982. 24 min. Multimedia Entertainment, $360.

This dramatization, aimed at children, shows a family in turmoil over a woman's increasing senility and the decision to move her to a nursing home. The talks between an eleven-year-old and her grandmother are exceptional.

Grandma's Been Arrested. 1983. 15 min. MTI Teleprograms, $275.

An excerpt from the "60 Minutes" television program follows the arrest and court appearance of an elderly shoplifter; the judge and Harry Reasoner discuss the rise in senior crime and the alternative sentencing and counseling programs available.

How to Spend Less Traveling and Enjoy It More (Consumer Reports series). 1986. 60 min. Lorimar Home Video, $19.95.

A plethora of travel information is presented in five easy-to-follow sections that give advice on how to plan and pack, travel-package buys, ticket shopping, health and safety, selecting the right travel agent, finding hotels, eating out and tipping, and exchanging currency.

Isaac in America: A Journey with Isaac Singer. 1985. 60 min. Amram Nowak Assoc., $350.

A journey through the past of this wonderful Yiddish storyteller celebrates his eightieth year and his fiftieth in America. Conducted by Singer himself, the tour retraces his first steps in America and shows the man still at work today, writing, translating, and joyously responding to modern audiences, whether in classrooms or at the Nobel Prize ceremony.

The Last Right. 1985. 29 min. New Dimension Films, $390.

A dramatic production that depicts how one family confronts the illness and death of an elderly relative. It raises ethical issues that surround family caregiving and explores the right of the elderly to choose how to live or die.

Miles to Go. 1984. 80 min. Filmakers Library, $500.

Eight women, ranging in age from twenty-seven to seventy-two, undertake a challenging and potentially dangerous two-week wilderness journey in the Great Smokey Mountains. This dramatic film portrays the group's dynamics, individual inspiration, and inner strength needed to accomplish a goal.

My Mother, My Father. 1984. 33 min. Terra Nova Films/New Dimension Films, $395.

A sensitive look at the problems of ailing, aging parents. Four actual situations are shown in this thought-provoking program about painful choices in a changing society.

Old Like Me. 1987. 27 min. Filmakers Library, $300.

Assuming the character of an eighty-five-year-old woman, Pat Moore, a twenty-six-year-old industrial designer, traveled through one hundred North American cities to experience firsthand the discrimination and barriers faced by elderly and disabled people.

Richard Simmons and the Silver Foxes. 1986. 45 min. Lorimar Home Video, $19.95.

Richard Simmons designed this special fitness plan for people over fifty. Parents of celebrities are led through a series of warm-up exercises, a low-impact, non-stress aerobic workout, and a three-minute relaxation session.

Silent Pioneers: Gay and Lesbian Elders. 1985. 42 min. Filmakers Library, $400.

A sensitive, insightful, and involving look at eight older Americans whose quiet homosexuality paved the way for a more open generation. A male couple together for fifty-five years, a black

great-grandmother, and a former monk turned rancher all talk
about the joys and sorrows of their lives.

Time Will Tell: Inner City Kids Rap with Elders. 1986. 16 min. Filmakers Library, $275.

This program shows the unlikely coming together of kids
from the New York school system, some of whom are targeted as
dropouts, and elderly residents of a nursing home. Acceptance,
love, and bolstered self-esteem are the result.

To Live until You Die. 1982. 50 min. Ambrose Video, $150.

Dr. Elisabeth Kübler-Ross, recognized expert in the field of
death and dying, clearly and affectingly discusses her experiences
helping the terminally ill face death without fear.

See also *On Death and Dying,* by Elisabeth Kübler-Ross
(page 45).

Chapter 12

Fiction

Fiction offers humor, inspiration, illumination, and escapism. Beyond the sheer pleasure of reading, a good novel is one way to deal with painful elements of life. Emotional and intellectual immersion in the lives of others (even invented characters) allows us to see how problems, such as ailing parents, widowhood, illness, or retirement, are resolved or complicated further. The latter may be just as enlightening. Many of the novels, such as those by Kingsley Amis and Hortense Calisher, are written by individuals with firsthand aging experience. In some stories, teens, children, and adult offspring are the prominent characters, and their relationships with grandparents and parents form the essence of the story. The vital influence of grandparents is wonderfully, honestly portrayed by showing how such a communion enriches both older and younger generations. The novels described are a select sampling of the endless array of beautiful, relevant books available.

These selections vary considerably—ranging from frivolous mystery stories and lighthearted novels to serious mysteries and wrenching novels. A general fiction section is followed by two genre sections: mysteries and espionage, then Westerns. Short stories provide the finale.

Novels

Adams, Alice. *Second Chances.* 1988. Knopf, $18.95.

> Adams begins her story in the 1980s, introducing Celeste, Polly, and two couples: Dudley and Sam, her husband, and Edward and his gay lover, Freddie. With grace and realistic turbulence, these old friends face the surprising prospect of their own aging. Polly is a puzzling, solitary woman—a sort of Robin Hood for the Mexican residents of their small town outside San Francisco. The

novel opens with Celeste adjusting to the death of her husband, Charlie, a renowned journalist and womanizer. Dudley and Sam, and Edward and Freddie are content, almost smug in the security of their own relationships. Smug enough, that is, to gossip mercilessly about the ifs and whys of Celeste's new boyfriend, Bill. The author returns to the past and writes a passage for each decade since 1945 to clarify and further entwine the interrelationships of these old friends. When Sara, the daughter of a longtime friend of Celeste, arrives, she is jokingly classified as "some sort of spy . . . gathering information on the habits of the old." The irony of this totally idle speculation by Dudley is that Sara does indeed draw the world of espionage into their lives. From a quite touching comedy on the manners, sexuality, and tragedies of aging, the novel moves into levels of suspense, with less success. This transition from private to international affairs does provide one final irony in the lives of these old friends.

Amis, Kingsley. *The Old Devils.* 1987. Summit, $18.95.

Amis's old devils are a collection of Welsh men and women reluctantly submitting to, or valiantly flailing against, the thought and reality of being old. As the novel opens, Charlie sets off for his daily Bible meeting. The Bible is the name of the pub where he meets Malcolm, Peter, and his other cronies. The news that sets off this particular gathering is the return of an old friend, Alun Weaver, and his wife, Rhiannon. Alun has made his living as a professional Welshman, trading upon the nostalgic perception the region holds for those outside it. The mysticism of Wales is by turns heralded and scoffed at. Alun is resented, yet his charisma cannot be denied (even by those wives who were once his lovers). The author writes so perceptively on the private problems of these men and women that it is almost embarrassing to know that Peter has been cast from the marital bed, that Charlie's bowel functions are his primary, perpetual concern, or that Garth must pay his wife for staying in her inherited home. Overall, the women are in much better physical and emotional condition, except for one troublesome alcoholic. The rigors of age have hit the men harder and they demonstrate little ability to spring back. While far from soothing, Amis's realistic fiction is imbued with humor and, surprisingly, romance.

Ariyoshi, Sawako. *The Twilight Years.* 1984. Kodansha, dist. by Harper, $16.95; paper, $5.95.

Ariyoshi has written a wrenching portrait of the struggles within a Japanese family as it copes pragmatically and emotionally with an aging parent. While the Japanese names, setting, and customs may at first seem difficult, the family quarrels, concerns, and affection are truly universal. Akiko Tachibana had never been a favorite of her curmudgeonly father-in-law, Shigezo. However, following the death of his wife and the onset of senility (possibly Alzheimer's disease although it is never diagnosed as such), Akiko is the only family member that Shigezo readily recognizes and will allow to care for him. She must sleep nearby, help him to the bathroom (and eventually change his diapers), bathe him, feed him, calm him, and even locate him when he runs off through the streets of Tokyo in a confused panic. As Shigezo's needs grow and his body becomes more fragile, Akiko is amazed to find that her initial frustration and impatience fade. She cares for him with growing devotion until she is the only person truly bereft when he dies. Akiko's husband's terror of aging inhibits him from participating in the blossoming relationship that evolves between this needy, weakening old man and his once-despised daughter-in-law. This was one of the first novels to graphically share the care of an elderly confused parent, and it remains the most powerful.

Brown, Rita Mae. *Bingo*. 1988. Bantam, $18.95.

In the small town of Runnymede, divided in half at the town square by the Mason-Dixon Line, old feuds are still rampant. Among these timeless squabbles is the sibling rivalry of the Hunsenmeir sisters (Julia and Louise), now in their eighties. Townspeople flock to the weekly bingo game at the Catholic church, not only for the prize money, but to witness the latest bout between the sisters. Their quarrels are escalated by the introduction of a new eligible man into the town. He dates first one sister, then the other, and they spy on each other's outings. Louise assumes an extraordinary spiritual pose to attract the suitor, while Julia dons falsies and tints her hair turquoise (only at the sides). Julia's daughter, Nickel Smith, is managing editor of the *Runnymede Clarion*, but she must spend a good deal of her time and energy arbitrating the ongoing battle between the octogenarian sisters. She often sides with Julia more through common sense than kinship. She is frequently summoned to the Curl'n' Twirl on Monday mornings when both ladies go to get their hair done. The shop owner, Mr. Pierre, arbitrates these encounters, but Nickel is often called away from the office for a significant revelation. Nickel Smith is a lesbian, yet is well-accepted in her hometown (probably because she has no female lover). The sisters' rivalry is really a sidelight to Nickel's attempt to maintain control over the newspaper and resolve an affair of her own. Brown's version of small-town life is filled with real emotions, hilarity, and wonderfully romantic coincidences.

Burns, Olive Ann. *Cold Sassy Tree.* 1984. Ticknor & Fields, $16.95; Dell, paper, $8.95.

Burns transports her audience to the turn of the century and the town of Cold Sassy, Georgia, through the tales, tall and true, of Will Tweedy. This fourteen-year-old can "always make a good story better in the telling." Mostly he tells about the remarriage of his grandfather, Rucker Blakeslee, within three weeks of the death of Will's treasured grandmother. Blakeslee's family and townspeople are appalled—particularly since his new bride is the hatmaker, Miss Love Simpson, a woman in her thirties with an unknown past. Will has a treasured friendship with his grandfather and is the only one in the family or town to accept his grandfather's new wife. The boy becomes the go-between for his mother and grandfather and consequently a good friend of Miss Simpson. The story is as filled with the mischief of the youth as it is with his perceptions on life, gleaned from his grandfather's actions and original—some would say heretical—sermons. Will sees the town's first automobile, cheats death as he clings to a train trestle, responds to his uncle's suicide, and learns about love through the evolving relationship of his grandfather and Miss Love. The perspective is that of a youth watching an old man become young. Blakeslee is the dominant figure in the town and the life of the novel.

Calisher, Hortense. *Age.* 1987. Weidenfield & Nicholson, $14.95.

Calisher's slim novel is a love story. Rupert and Gemma are a married couple in their seventies and have agreed to compose an almanac so that the survivor will be left a record of final thoughts as a measure of comfort. Calisher fills her novel with a level of tension that goes beyond Gemma and Rupert's curiosity about who will die first and how the survivor will cope. Rupert's ex-wife suddenly appears. She is terminally ill, yet a presence that can intervene in the second marriage of her former husband. An element of suspense is introduced in the effect this woman will exert upon Rupert's and Gemma's lives and their still exquisitely intimate marriage. A lesson is learned by both Gemma and Rupert. As the novel closes, the couple are no longer preparing for death, but planning their future. Calisher's lovely, genuine novel may do more for testifying to the continued sexuality of older people than the assertions set down by Consumer Reports (in the report *Love, Sex, and Aging,* page 27).

Carillo, Charles. *Shepherd Avenue.* 1986. Atlantic Monthly Pr., $15.95.

The Ambrosios have not been a close family. Joey has met his grandparents, Angelo and Connie, only once before his father, shattered by the death of his wife, quits his job and leaves his only son with them. It is 1961 and ten-year-old Joey is unaccustomed to the ethnic city neighborhood where his father grew up. Angelo, Connie, and their teenage son Vic cope awkwardly with this angry, distant youngster. Joey's adjustments to a new family, neighborhood, friends, and religion and his impact on this family is fascinating. After Angelo "slips into retirement" he and Joey become friends. Joey notices, "Connie had barely adjusted to having me around . . . then there was Angie observing her go about her daily routines with the curiosity of a school kid watching a lion tamer." Angelo's closest friend dies and Joey's moves away. Their common grief sets them on "the verge of a friendship." When Joey stakes a claim to his grandfather as friend, Angelo exclaims, "Friend? I'm your blood!" One other link between grandfather and grandson is, sadly, their common enmity with the dictatorial, abrasive Connie. This willful woman is never understood. Despite the tragedies and few buoyant moments they share, Joey feels only a "twinge of compassion" for her. With his flair for detail and the intense realism of his people, Carillo moves the reader right into this New York City neighborhood. Joey's growing bond with his grandfather and ceaseless hostility toward his grandmother are only two of the many powerful elements of this rewarding story.

Dorfman, Ariel. *Widows.* 1984. Penguin, paper, $7.95.

Dorfman, a Chilean citizen in exile, contrived an elaborate charade in order to secure publication of this politically charged novel in his own country. He wished to write of "the disappearance of thousands of men, and some women, into the hands of the secret police of dictatorships." So he wrote as if he were a European, Eric Lohmann, decrying and describing events in Greece earlier in this century. The possibility for the translation and distribution of a foreign novel in South America is much greater than the original publication of a local work. His plan was foiled; but this remarkable fiction is all the more intriguing for its hidden realities. In a small village filled with the wives (widows?) of men who have been hauled away by the military, a corpse is washed up on the riverbank where the women do their laundry. It is claimed by a strong-minded woman, Sofia Angelo, as the body of her husband. The acceptance of her husband's death would end the painful limbo of doubt and fear over his continued existence in a wretched prison. The military in control of this small town would prefer to bury the body anonymously, fearing that a funeral ceremony would spark an uprising against martial law. Their attempted suppression of this woman's mantle of widowhood results in a coalition. Thirty-seven women claim the faceless corpse. Each demands that the military offer proof that her husband is not a corpse; that is, deliver some evidence of his continued existence. The strength of this political revolt led by an aging woman who heads a household of three generations is impressive. Dorfman illustrates how the call for widowhood becomes a political force—a conspiracy on the surface but in reality a plea for truth and decency. The women are asking: are we widows? and why? It makes a stunning story.

Edgerton, Clyde. *Walking across Egypt.* 1987. Algonquin, $14.95; Ballantine, paper, $3.95; G. K. Hall Large Print Books, $16.95.

Edgerton's heroine is Mattie Rigsbee, age seventy-eight, who cooks and dreams as she hums the hymn her father once sang to her, "Walking across Egypt." Mattie finds a stray hound on her porch, feeds it, as she does everyone (human or animal) who stops by, then calls the dogcatcher. Her son Robert, age forty-three, suggests she keep the animal. Tactfully, she does not tell this unmarried son that she yearns to be a grandmother, not a dog owner. Her response is, "I'm slowing down. I got as much business keeping a dog as I do walking across Egypt." By the novel's end, though, she has taken on responsibilities far more taxing than caring for a stray dog. It is the appearance of the dogcatcher, Lamar Benfield, as well as Mattie's propensity to invite anyone and everyone to dinner, that get her involved with shielding a fugitive. Edgerton creates some wildly humorous, nearly slapstick, scenes as he demonstrates Mattie's ability to laugh at and love life. This tendency strains her relations with her children and at times creates turmoil in her church. She is a character to be admired in a purely enjoyable novel.

Flagg, Fannie. *Fried Green Tomatoes at the Whistle Stop Café.* 1987. Random, $17.95; McGraw-Hill, paper, $5.95.

Flagg fills her boisterous novel with the heart and soul of a small town—merely a whistle stop on the train line outside Birmingham, Alabama—before and shortly after the Second World War. Characters named Idgie (short for Imogene) and Wonderful Counsel highlight her tale. It is most enlivened by the passionate

Idgie, who forms friendships regardless of color, sex, or reputation and keeps them for life—even at the risk of her own. Along with sheer zaniness, a tense foreboding fills the tale from the beginning when Vinnie first drops hints of a murder trial. Vinnie is Mrs. Cleo Threadgoode and a link in Flagg's unusual story-telling chain. Flagg tells her story through bits of narrative linked by bulletins from a gossipy town newsletter produced by Dot Weems and by the recollections of Mrs. Threadgoode uttered (forty years later) in a nursing home. By the novel's end there emerges a story of abduction, murder, and local justice. Vinnie's audience is a depressed, menopausal visitor, Evelyn Couch, whose life is transformed by these Sunday afternoon chats. She much prefers Vinnie's nostalgic and common-sense talks to the whining of her mother-in-law who resides down the hall. Evelyn experiences a marvelous rejuvenation by listening carefully to Mrs. Threadgoode's life stories.

Fleming, Berry. *Who Dwelt by a Churchyard.* 1989. Permanent Press (Noyak Rd., Sag Harbor, NY 11963), $18.95.

Fleming, at age eighty-nine, composed a short, stream-of-consciousness novel. This fictitious memoir features Allen Embry, currently in the process of "transferring his aloneness to simpler quarters." Resigned to leaving his home to live with his divorced daughter, Embry reviews his life as he sorts through old photographs. The result is a prickly tale of Embry's loves, regrets, and sorrows. A recent widower, he reads a bewildering, unfinished letter left behind by his wife. In it she refers to Embry as "that stranger she married in another life." His aching grief is intensified by this puzzling missive never intended for his eyes. Fleming's novel can be confusing as his character jumps from youthful days in Paris to the recent past. The author's style simulates life-review—the common pattern of reminiscence experienced by elderly people—with such realism that it should strike a familiar chord. Many of Fleming's earlier novels have been reissued and well-received. These include *Colonel Effingham's Raid, Siesta,* and *Lucinderella.*

Hodges, Hollis. *Norman Rockwell's Greatest Painting.* 1988. Erikson, $16.95.

In Hodges' comic, romantic novel Ebert Olney is a widower who has bought a small apartment residence in Stockbridge, Massachusetts—once home and inspiration to Norman Rockwell. This affable, extremely ordinary older man would easily fit into one of Rockwell's paintings. Actually, in Hodges' story, many of the people around Olney have been painted by Rockwell. Several have appeared in a previously unknown Rockwell painting that a local politician plans to unveil to kick off his campaign. Among Olney's tenants is Brenda, a gossip collector who plans to string local facts and hearsay into a sensational novel. She shares far more of her findings with Olney than he wishes to hear. As a result, Olney becomes embroiled in the troubles of his tenants and neighbors. He uses this information to great advantage, subtly swaying the fate of his new friends. It seems there is no one else to enliven Olney's lonely days, except perhaps Dr. Whooter. Hodges writes about an older woman, Mary, in a nearby town whose attention has been caught by a spoofish self-help guide on sex and aging. The serio-comic advice of Dr. Whooter guides Mary and Olney into a whirlwind romance. Admittedly less than believable, especially with the neat happy endings for all concerned, the tale does a lovely job of poking fun at "how to gray gracefully guides" while divining the fate of some lovely characters.

Inman, Robert. *Home Fires Burning*. 1987. Little, Brown, $17.95; Ballantine, paper, $4.95.

Inman has created a stunning story set in a small southern town during World War II. The home fires are kept burning by the old and young while the war is fought. Among the most vocal of these tenders is Jake Tibbets, the local newspaper editor, owner, and publisher. Jake, his friends, fellow townspeople, and relatives are introduced with such heartfelt detail that the reader becomes part of the community. Five generations of the Tibbets family are featured in this tale, but Jake and his grandson Lonnie are the central figures. On trips to the woods Lonnie speaks to the ghost of an ancestor from the Civil War, Captain Finley Tibbets. The young boy reenacts the hero's battles and consults the Captain's spirit on critical matters that he cannot pursue with his grandfather. Jake is wrestling with the demons of his father's weak spirit which he sees reappearing in his own son (Lonnie's father). These family consultations add depth to a riotously funny novel. One of Jake's most interesting struggles is faced as the war ends and the next generation returns to take charge of the community. Jake's inability to relinquish his power forces him to reexamine his life. Inman is a wonderful storyteller who has incorporated universal questions within an irresistible historical novel.

Jolley, Elizabeth. *Mr. Scobie's Riddle*. 1984. Viking, $13.95.

Jolley is an Australian author whose fiction displays a sardonic view of life. Her novel opens in the form of memos between matron Hyacinth Price and the night sister of the Hospital of St. Christopher and St. Jude for the elderly. These memos reveal that the care is far from excellent with confusion a familiar state to both staff and patients. The hospital, actually a private nursing home, has Martin Scobie as a new, unwilling patient. Mr. Scobie complains to his nephew that, "There's no dignity at C & J." It is a wacky place with a select patient grouping. He meets Mr. Hughes who sneaks off to smoke saying, "It is no use to make life longer without life." The matron's goal is not longevity; rather she encourages her patients' disorientation and confusion. When apparently hearty patients disappear one-by-one, Mr. Scobie tries to escape. He is recovered every time and his name moves closer to the top of the matron's list. This list consists of patients with property that can be signed over to her or the institution. Mr. Scobie's riddle is, "What is it that we all know is going to happen, but we don't know when or how?" In this sinister, darkly comic tale it could be anything anywhere.

Kupfer, Fern. *Surviving the Seasons.* 1987. Delacorte, $17.95.

Life in the senior citizen condominiums of Florida for Jake and Sara, Harry and June, and Herbie and Betty has its share of ups and downs. Kupfer draws the reader into a caring, pensive relationship with these seniors who are definitely not caricatures or retirees from real life—their passions, boredom, adjustments, and woes are real. The novelist fills out their lives with flashbacks to the early days of their marriages when their children were small people requiring care. Now these adult offspring are fussing over their parents as if aging has suddenly made them helpless and taken decision-making out of their hands and into those of their children. One widowed woman finds herself overburdened with company and intruded upon by well-intentioned family and friends. Kupfer's soft-spoken writing manages to be both realistic and romantic. The sensitivity to the older parent's perspective makes this a novel with multi-generational appeal.

Littlefield, Bill. *Prospect.* 1989. Houghton Mifflin, $17.95.

A retired baseball scout, Pete Estey, sits in a rest home wasting his talents and energies until an aide, Louise Brown, draws him out of his doldrums and away from the home. Louise (who is also in her seventies) invites Pete to use her spare room after a fire at the residence makes his room uninhabitable. She has an ulterior motive, as her grandnephew, Jack, is a powerful baseball pitcher. Despite Estey's muttered disavowals, she is certain

that he can help Jack get noticed by the major leagues. Baseball talk fills Estey's recollections and the descriptions of Jack's hometown games. The story, alternately narrated by Louise and Estey, illustrates their differing perspectives on one another, the events in the novel, and life in general. Louise, a very upbeat person, maintains a running conversation with the Lord. Estey, by contrast, is a disillusioned soul. The comic aspects of life in the rest home are nicely rendered, as are the trials on the baseball field and in the manager's offices. Definitely a sentimental novel, it will strike the hearts of many readers, especially baseball fans.

McCoy, Maureen. *Summertime*. 1987. Poseidon, $15.95; Washington Square Pr., paper, $6.95.

Jessamine Morrow's elopement with Hazen Batten from the Hillcrest Retirement Center serves as a catalyst in the staid lives of her daughter-in-law and granddaughter. Alice, the fifty-six-year-old widow of James Lawrence Morrow (Jessamine's son), wears her chestnut hair in a perfect bun and lives nearly buried in craft items she has uncovered in her job as a buyer for a catalog company. She "felt done with the man/woman thing, truly deep, deep bone-weary done." Her exhaustion stems from supporting James through a long-term illness which ended fifteen months earlier. Alice and her daughter, Carla, are astounded that Jessamine has remarried at eighty-five. Carla lives in a haven in the woods with her husband, Brian, a lockkeeper on the Mississippi River. With her back-to-nature demeanor she is seeking refuge and pursuing the "Morrow

wisdom: the less you do, the safer you are." But the eldest Morrow's brave encounter with a new spouse eventually prompts all three to accept new risks and challenges. When Carla discovers she is pregnant, she dashes panic-stricken to her mother. Together they share beautiful days and finally recover from their grief over James. The novelist draws the everyday adventures of these three women in such colorful detail that the nursing home residents, Alice's cluttered house and empty love life, and Carla's brave façades and real fears turn into lovely lessons on living, ever so subtly taught.

Novick, Marian. *At Her Age*. 1986. Scribner's, $15.95; G. K. Hall Large Print Books, $16.95.

Weary of wheelchair and walker races to the lunchroom, unproductive craft classes, and geriatric nutrition lectures, Molly Vorobey, age seventy-five, decides to flee the protective confines of Miami's Wallace A. Dalton Senior Citizens' Complex and head home to New York City. The novelist intersperses Molly's present-day adventures with those of her youth, starting with her childhood immigration from Russia and leading up to the recent years of tension with her daughter, Sheila. Carriage rides in Central Park, lunch in the Russian Tea Room, and shopping at Bloomingdale's occupy Molly's first day of freedom. It all seems blissful until she is mugged. Too stubborn to call her daughter, who has by now hired a private detective to find her errant mother, Molly calls her grandson, Justin, a student at Columbia University. After considerable coaxing, Justin offers his grandmother refuge—in his all-male dormitory. Molly and Justin's friends enjoy some intense cross-generational conversations over pizza and beer. Justin, whose studies and sex life have become hampered by this popular visitor, tries to effect a reconciliation between his mother and grandmother. The result is a farcical meeting at a museum—by far the most absurdly comic moment in a novel filled with light satire, brash humor, poignant memories, and sensitive perceptions on aging and family ties.

Rowntree, Kathleen. *The Haunting of Willow Dasset.* 1989. Little, Brown, $17.95.

Rowntree has written a heartrending, buoyant story about a young girl's idyllic summers spent at her grandfather's farm. As a child, Sally helps with the harvest, runs through the fields, and revels in her grandfather's love. Even though it is told from the granddaughter's perspective, the narrative will bring warmth and enlightenment to older readers as well. Sally, as a young girl, feels that her days spent at Willow Dasset Farm are as close to perfect happiness as one could imagine. Each successive summer dulls that shining vision because Sally's maturation brings on new family tensions and enables her to perceive other, barely dormant rifts and rivalries. Sally awakens to her grandfather's limitations, and is further inhibited by the jealousy of an unmarried aunt. Living nearby in mild but increasing chaos are three other elderly aunts and an uncle who are dear to Sally and dreaded by her father. Great-aunt Pip's flirtatious nature is a bane for the overly reserved man. Rowntree comically yet kindly exploits these older characters, adding depth and zest to her family tale. The contrasting approaches of old and young to aging and to the imminence of death are sensitively plumbed in this bittersweet novel.

Santmyer, Helen Hooven. . . . *And Ladies of the Club.* 1984. Putnam, $19.95.

Santmyer was eighty-eight years old when her novel of over 1,100 pages was published. From her nursing home, the author relished the public acclaim her book received, even if much of it focused on her years rather than her writing style. She had been at work on it for fifty years and the time span of the story also covers five decades. She tells about the lives of a set of close friends from the close of the Civil War through the Great Depression. Sally Rausch and Anne Gordon marry Civil War heroes in 1868 and eventually form the Waynesboro Ladies Literary Society. The lives of these ladies, other club members, and their spouses provide plenty of turmoil to sustain a novel of such length. Watching the changing moral and cultural landscape along with significant moments in history through the eyes of these ordinary people provides a memorable fictional sojourn. The word "ordinary" would undoubtedly offend Santmyer since her original intention was to free the reader from the mundane image of small-town life as described by Sinclair Lewis in *Main Street*. Santmyer's story is filled with old-fashioned charm.

Shaw, Robert W. *Abbott and Avery*. 1987. Viking, $16.95.

Wesley Abbott finds himself driving through town at 3:00 a.m. to quiet his howling grandson, Avery. How did he get himself into such a situation? His wife has left him to explore her artistic dimensions; his daughter (Heath, the infant's mother) must finish college to ensure her own independence; Lew, the baby's father, is willing to marry Heath, but is ineffectual at combating her objections. She insists Lew must "do something adventurous that will enrich us as a couple, for later." That leaves Abbott with rides at 3:00 in the morning, steamy bathrooms to soothe croupy coughs, and far too many sick days from his job as a newspaper editor and columnist. Abbott's boss calls for something funny about grandfatherhood, but Abbott takes his job as parent too seriously to comply. The novelist stretches Abbott's attempts to comprehend Avery a bit far, especially when the grandfather imitates the baby's gurgles, fetal position, and manhandling of apple mush. The story contains a lot more than the fun and practicalities of baby care. Abbott's concern for Avery nearly destroys the family that he is trying to hold together when he refuses to let go. Meanwhile, Abbott must also make appearances at the office, look out for an old friend whose life is falling apart, and contemplate the state of his own marriage. Shaw carries off the often corny, truly affecting trek into the insides of this character's emotional life—fatherhood, marriage, friendship, career, and grandfatherhood—with humor and sincerity.

Small, David. *The River in Winter*. 1987. Norton, $16.95.

This grandfather-grandson story is grisly and even terrifying. Small redeems his fatalistic novel by the sheer grit of his two central characters, Henry Weatherfield and his grandson, Joe. Weatherfield blames the family's ongoing troubles on his own experiences in the Second World War. When he shot a young German soldier, Henry asserts, "the bullet traveled on" bringing misfortune to the Weatherfield family for generations. It certainly seems true for Henry's grandson, Joe. As a teenager evicted by a brutal stepfather, Joe seeks refuge at his grandfather's house where he finds a surly drunk spouting classical literature. Small writes with harsh clarity about the slowly growing intimacy between this alcoholic doctor and stubborn heir to the family's failings. Every well-intentioned act by Joe is fatally misconstrued—his struggle to rescue his mother from her sadistic spouse, his heroic intervention in a kidnapping/hostage situation, and even his attempts to pull his grandfather out of a life of solitary dissipation—all become the stuff of tragedy. This is a difficult story, but it is not as desperately unhappy as this summary makes it seem. At times, Joe rises beyond his own anger at life and the family heritage of failure. Small does a masterful job in presenting a young man's frustrations and, most of all, the potent influence that a grandson and grandfather can exert upon one another.

Wesley, Mary. *Jumping the Queue.* 1988. Penguin, $6.95.
Wesley, Mary. *Not That Sort of Girl.* 1988. Viking, $17.95.

Wesley was in her seventies when she published her first novel in 1983. As a widow of modest means she no longer had the luxury of debating whether her fiction was fit for publication (according to an interview in a London newspaper, "For years she wrote stories but always threw them away because she thought they were no good"). What a loss. She has published five splendid novels since 1983. The two titles cited above feature reflections and plans of recently widowed women.

In *Jumping the Queue*, Matilda Poliport has planned an elegant suicide. She has packed a picnic lunch to eat before a final swim in the ocean. Her plans are foiled when she rescues a younger man who is sought by the police for the murder of his mother. The loving relationship that evolves between Hugh and Matilda is uncanny, yet quite plausibly developed. His presence as listener draws out troubles she has suppressed with her children and her perfect husband. Matilda explains about her children's infrequent visits: "I could see my grief bored them. Mothers are not supposed to be in love with your father—there's something indecent about it." Much more acerbic visions of the way older individuals are viewed and treated by the young fill this novel. It is equally packed with adventure—hints of espionage, incest, adultery, drug smuggling, and so on, although some of these elements clutter rather than enhance the story. The way that Wesley details the characters of Matilda and Hugh is intriguing, but the most sustaining of all is Matilda's humor, courage, and eccentricity.

Not That Sort of Girl is a more congenial story that touches upon aging with subtlety. A recent widow, Rose, retires to a country inn to reflect upon her stable, comfortable marriage and her lifelong love affair with another man. Through private reminiscences, this apparently docile woman reveals depths unplumbed by her husband or her ingratiating, snooty neighbors—a pair of twins who have exercised a lifelong tendency to annoy and take advantage of Rose. Her final, romantic triumph leaves them baffled, but the reader feels as blissful as Rose. Wesley demonstrates a wily imagination and an ability to create characters that readily tug at the heart and mind. Rose's relations with her son, her own parents, and her in-laws serve as the novel's backdrop. Her recollections are largely scenarios of her formidable handling of the family's country home and farms during the Second World War. In this way, Wesley fills in the portrait of Rose's life far more realistically than she does for Matilda Poliport. Even though they differ sharply, both are appealing, wryly humorous novels.

Wolitzer, Hilma. *Silver*. 1988. Farrar, $8.95.

Paulette and Howard Flax's silver wedding anniversary is approaching. She is determined not to celebrate the twenty-fifth anniversary of marital vows that Howard has not upheld. One night her husband's moans interrupt Paulie's plans for independence. Paulie is dismayed by his sexual timing; but it is pain, not arousal, that Howard is expressing. He has had a heart attack. So instead of establishing a new life for herself, Paulie must rush him to the hospital, then nurse him back to health. The incident leaves Howard even more in love with his wife (and determined to end his affair). Paulie is even more determined to leave. This story of marital crisis is told by both spouses in alternate chapters, but the novelist's compassion is obviously with the betrayed wife. The schism in the Flaxes' marriage is exacerbated but finally resolved by their son Jason's relationship with his girlfriend. Her premarital pregnancy and Jason's reluctance to marry evoke vivid recollections by both Howard and Paulie of their own tumultuous courtship and rushed marriage. Wolitzer draws this family quandary with appropriate humor, zestful characters, and touching reconciliations.

Mysteries and Espionage

Ferrars, E. X. *A Murder Too Many*. 1989. Doubleday, $14.95.

Ferrars has written more than fifty mysteries and her amateur detective, botany professor Andrew Basnett, has starred in many of them. Basnett, age seventy-two, has been retired for five years and widowed for ten. He decides to attend a professional conference at Knotlington University where he first taught. His arrival summons fond memories of his early university years, especially of fun shared with his wife Nell. Soon Basnett has little time for reminiscing or botany as he is asked by the wife of a murdered man to investigate the case. Basnett dissents, but is soon caught up in the puzzle since old friends are involved. The murder of resident artist Carl Judd, a notorious philanderer, has unsettled this quiet community. Even more upsetting was the conviction of a well-liked young professor, Stephen Sharland, who was seen leaving the scene of the crime in a blood-stained cardigan. Judd's wife believes in Sharland's innocence and soon Basnett does too. Proof is difficult to come by, especially since the case is officially closed and the botanist has no professional status. His unassuming nature allows him entry into the homes and access to the hidden natures of people involved. Basnett occasionally mentions the limitations (or virtues) of being over seventy, but his age is not a matter of amazement or humor, just a fact.

Gilman, Dorothy. *Mrs. Pollifax and the Golden Triangle.* 1988. Doubleday, $15.95.

Emily Pollifax was first introduced in Gilman's novel, *The Unexpected Mrs. Pollifax* (Doubleday, 1966), in which she decided to apply in person to work at the CIA and, remarkably enough, was accepted. After all, as a garden club chairwoman and widowed mother of two grown children, her cover was impeccable (her brown belt in karate was an impressive reference, too). As this eighth adventure opens, the heroine is still recovering from her last assignment and planning a simple, relaxing vacation to Thailand with her new husband, Curtis Reed. Their plans are slightly altered when Mr. Carstairs, Emily's CIA boss, receives a cryptic message from a mysterious operative in a small Thai village. Mr. Carstairs asks the pair of senior citizens to pose as tourists and pick up an innocuous-looking parcel containing significant political information. The job, of course, is not so smoothly accomplished. Is it because Emily craves adventure or attracts it? Anyway, Curtis is kidnapped and Emily spends days in pursuit of his captors slogging through the jungle with a fearsome-looking smuggler. As they are eluding border patrols, bandits, and natural dangers, they find a mysterious American, posing as a photojournalist, who resembles a missing, high-ranking CIA official. Gilman, highly skilled at pacing her fiction, sets off surprising dangers and coincidences to the very end. For retirees considering foreign travel, Mrs. Pollifax-Reed sets quite an example.

Langton, Jane. *Good and Dead.* 1986. St. Martin's, $15.95; Penguin, paper, $3.95.

"This is a story about too many funerals in a single church." Langton, a poised mystery author, has taken difficult topics— euthanasia, Alzheimer's disease, religious faith, and marital infidelity—and neatly woven them into a darkly comic, enticing novel. Langton wastes little time dropping extraneous clues. She lets readers in on the reasons for the sudden decline in the parish rosters of the Old West Church and leaves them to fret over whether Homer Kelly, former district attorney of Middlesex County, and others will discover the truth. The most obvious crisis involves the plight of the new minister and his wife. From their first appearance in the church, "it was obvious that Claire Bold was not long for this world." With the Reverend Bold in such torment, other members step in to help. Among them is Ed Bell, who arranges Sunday afternoon meetings for terminally ill church members. Variously described as prayer sessions, hymnal selection studies, or Bible classes, the actual purpose of the meetings is to discuss the morality as well as the practicalities of euthanasia. The attendees, who have kept the seriousness of their health problems secret from their spouses and neighbors, should have been as discreet about Bell's meetings. As participants decline in number, people become suspicious of Ed Bell, "that stalwart pillar of the church." When the sheriff refuses to investigate, his querulous wife deputizes herself and demands action from Homer Kelly. This congregation of good men and women proves to be as filled with virtuous, avaricious, helpful, grieving, and justified people as any other group—although perhaps a bit more edged with intrigue.

le Carré, John. *The Quest for Karla: Tinker, Tailor, Soldier, Spy; The Honourable Schoolboy; Smiley's People.* 1982. Knopf, $13.95.

Le Carré, a renowned espionage writer, features George Smiley, a dynamic, persistent, elderly British agent, in some of his most famous novels. *The Quest for Karla* is not a specific story; instead it is a title given to the trilogy of novels cited above that are also available individually in various paperback, hardcover, and large-print editions. This particular volume is mentioned so that all three books may be easily discussed. Those unfamiliar with le Carré's writing may still know George Smiley from the made-for-TV movies created from *Tinker, Tailor, Soldier, Spy* and *Smiley's People*. In the first story, George Smiley is called out of retirement to smoke out a double agent within British intelligence. One of their top men turns out to be a counter agent who has been operating in their midst for years. In the later novels, the British agency has lost credibility due to the effectiveness of Smiley's work. Smiley is asked to retire quietly as if it were he, not the traitor, who brought this ignominy. Smiley refuses, and when a fellow agent is murdered enroute to hand him some vital information, he returns to the field. The success of this older agent may not be duplicated by all of le Carré's readers as they wend their way through his exasperatingly challenging puzzles to ferret out the true villains and their methods.

MacLeod, Charlotte. *The Recycled Citizen*. 1988. Mysterious Pr., $15.95.

Adolphus and Mary Kelling, enormously wealthy like all of the Kellings, have developed a recycling center that serves as much as a community center as it does a place where impoverished seniors can turn in collected bottles and cans for cash. Their plans for a housing development for these homeless seniors look doomed when murder and charges of heroin smuggling (in pop cans planted on the elderly collectors) lead to Adolphus's arrest. MacLeod once again employs the eccentricities of the entire Kelling clan to produce a solution to an outlandish murder. Surrounded by great-uncles, aunts, and cousins, Sara is the most youthful of the clan. Her sensible husband, a private detective in the art world, orchestrates the investigation. Fortunately, family wiles triumph over a greedy villain. MacLeod creates delightful characters and some great leads (and dead ends) in the plot's puzzle. In this, MacLeod's seventh Sarah Kelling mystery, the elderly relatives continue to play a lively—though mostly humorous—role.

Mortimer, John. *Rumpole's Return*. 1982. Penguin, paper, $3.95.

British barrister Harold Rumpole is probably better known from the public television series than from Mortimer's fiction. While the screen performance divulges the full range of his idiosyncrasies, the print version allows one to revel in Rumpole's language. The barrister's down-to-earth legal opinions are interspersed with classical quotations and amusing mutterings about his wife, who is referred to in undertones as "she who must be obeyed." She is a dithery soul who possesses a necessary iron streak. In this novel she has somehow convinced Rumpole to retire to Florida and join their only son in his lovely, suburban home. Her incessant coaxing was only half the impetus. A series of negative verdicts from a judge who has been incessantly on Rumpole's case finally convinced him to leave his beloved profession. Rumpole finds retirement a trial. The Englishman is miserable in Florida until a casual inquiry from a former coworker sends him dashing back to work. The suspense of whether or not Rumpole can solve the case is only half the mystery; the other is how he will disentangle himself from his Floridian commitment and regain his office space. Rumpole's perceptions on America's retirement haven are fun to observe.

O'Marie, Carol Anne. *The Missing Madonna*. 1988. Doubleday/ Delacorte, $15.95.

O'Marie, herself a nun, has written two previous mysteries starring her seventy-year-old sleuths, Sister Mary Helen and Sister Eileen. As this story opens the nuns are attending an OWLS (Older Women's League) convention with several other old friends. The women are college alumnae who keep in close contact with one another despite their widely varying lifestyles. Truly they are as different as possible, which lends color (and a few off-color remarks) to the action. When their friend Erma fails to show up for the convention, they're puzzled. Bewilderment turns to genuine concern when, upon their return to San Francisco, Erma seems to have vanished. It seems wholly out of character for her to vanish with no word to her grown children or her friends. The OWLS adhere to their motto, "Organize, don't agonize," and the women meet in Erma's apartment with her rather troublesome offspring to start a search. Sister Mary Helen's assignment is to pray. In response to this tame mission, she misquotes, "Prayer without good works is dead," and sets off on her own dangerous style of sleuthing. The old (one of the author's frequent terms) detective nuns lend novelty to this mild suspense story in which humor outshines the mystery.

Sawyer, Corinne Holt. *The J. Alfred Prufrock Murders*. 1988. Donald I. Fine, $17.95; Fawcett Crest, paper, $3.50.

When Angela Benbow, an admiral's widow, decided to move to Camden-sur-Mer, a retirement hotel and cottage community, she had no idea that she would take up sleuthing along with handi-crafts. Sawyer's feisty, seventyish heroine had always stepped on a lot of toes with her frank opinions and forthright responses. It is no different at Camden. But for her fortunate friendship with three tolerant women, Angela may have been ostracized, if not murdered. When a quiet ex-librarian from Duluth is found fatally stabbed near the beach, Angela and her friends decide to launch their own investigation. Some residents judge this to be a tasteless new pas-time or just a new excuse for sharing gossip. In any event, it works. The klutzy searches, tittering brainstorming sessions, and serious tête-à-têtes with the handsome police detective are drawn by Saw-yer with just enough coyness, feasibility, and enthusiasm. Angela learns the villain's identity, and along the way learns to keep some of her villainous remarks to herself. The novel makes an engaging whodunit as well as a low-key lesson on the social proprieties and hazards of senior community living.

Thomas, Craig. *Wildcat*. 1989. Putnam, $19.95; Berkley/Jove, paper, $4.95.

In this riveting espionage novel, Thomas has major charac-ters in their sixties and seventies fighting for their families as well as their countries. Sir Kenneth Aubrey of British intelligence is forced into a confrontation with archfoes Brigitte Winterbach and Andrew Babbington. Aubrey proved Babbington to be a double agent and is still tainted by the scandal that rocked England (told in Thomas's earlier novel, *Lion's Run*). Determined not to retire, Aubrey is given one greater reason to work. Brigitte in East Berlin and Babbington in Moscow are directing a masterful plot to en-snare the government of Nepal. Aubrey's ward, Timothy Gardiner, has witnessed suspicious Soviet activity in that tiny nation where he is regretfully closing Britain's Gurkha units. When Aubrey, in an unrelated incident, witnesses the death of Brigitte's grown son, she turns all her attention to vengeance. Gardiner in Nepal is a perfect target. Engrossing, if a bit unrealistic, scenes of Gardiner eluding his assassins in the streets and mountains of Nepal alter-nate with chapters tracking the distant Aubrey's dogged espionage and rescue operation. As he struggles to prove Gardiner worthy of assistance by British intelligence, flashbacks of his earlier encoun-ters with Brigitte expose the truth of their relationship. Since Tho-mas so clearly fills in the essential details, it is not necessary to return to his earlier books *Wolfbane* (1978) and *Lion's Run* (1985); however, his exciting style may convince one to do so. This complicated adventure is first-rate espionage fiction, enhanced by the long-term relationships and lifetime experience of the major spies.

Wilhelm, Kate. *The Hamlet Trap*. 1987. St. Martin's, $15.95.

Wilhelm is a terrific science fiction novelist and all-round fiction writer. This book marks the start of a new mystery series starring Charlie Meiklejohn and his wife, Constance Leidl. Charlie is a retired New York City policeman turned private investigator, and Constance is a renowned psychologist whose insight into human nature is a definite help to Charlie's new career. Equally advantageous is their loving, friendly relationship that brightens the novel and the characters' spirits when a case looks particularly nasty. Wealthy grandparents concerned about the fate of a grand-daughter (Ginnie) they have not seen in two decades (since the death of their only son) summon the detective team from their east coast country house to solve a murder in Seattle. Wilhelm opens the novel by immersing the reader in the closed, frantic life of a small, prosperous repertory theater company. The murder suspect is Ginnie, an impressive set designer who is also the theater owner's niece. Wilhelm expertly draws the reader into the life of the theater and the concerns of all the crew. Such intimacy only extends the confusion over who actually did commit murder, and why. Clues are discovered but not easily connected. The skills and personalities of both Charlie and Constance are so well-utilized that, by the novel's end, Wilhelm has created anticipation for their next appearance.

Westerns

Cooke, John Byrne. *South of the Border*. 1989. Bantam, $17.95.

Cooke writes this Western in the voice of a man in his sixties, Charles Siringo, a retired Pinkerton agent and cowboy who had pursued Butch Cassidy and now, in the 1920s, owns a bunk-house in the new town called Hollywood. In his memoir, Siringo recalls his days with a small independent movie company and their travels to Mexico to make one of the earliest full-length motion pictures. The staff consists of a rough rodeo company and includes Charlie's daughter, the star, Victoria Hartford. Charlie and an apparently trustworthy drifter named Leroy Roberts accompany the movie-makers as payroll guards. The plot calls for the lovely Victoria to be carried off by Pancho Villa and rescued by the movie's hero and his pals. Although it seems too obvious for Cooke to write a story in which this plot would be duplicated in the real life of the movie company, he does and it works. Daring scenes show bravery, warfare, and cunning battle tactics. One thing that keeps the story alive is how the line between villain and hero is obscured and altered by the circumstances. Charlie realizes that Leroy, once pegged an outlaw and chased by Pinkerton agents, makes a valuable companion. At the same time, Leroy's friendship with Villa alternately rescues and endangers the movie company. Beyond Charlie's references to himself as an old cowboy and his excessive tendency to sermonize, there is little evidence that he has aged. His recollections add color to this intricately detailed novel filled with shoot-em-up scenes, romance, and a new perspective on the afterlife of Butch Cassidy.

Dodd, Susan. *Mamaw.* 1988. Viking, $18.95.

Dodd's historical novel is riddled with compassion and shattering drama. It tells the fictionalized life story of Zerelda Cole James Samuel, mother of Jesse James and seven others. Since it starts from her childhood, this novel may seem an unlikely selection for these stories on aging; yet this fierce, devoted woman faced widowhood, the death of a treasured son, and another husband's senility, to name only a few of the adversities she endured. As the wife of Reverend Robert James she gave birth to Frank, Jesse, and Sallie. Her marriage to Dr. Reuben Samuel brought five more children to the Missouri farm. As the oldest boys matured, the horrors of the Civil War encroached upon the James/Samuel farm, including the attempted lynching of Samuel by Union soldiers. Zerelda is convinced that his mind took to wandering from this trauma. Jesse's and Frank's outlaw lives are placed in perspective against the atrocities of the war, especially the legally ordained ones, such as the family's exile from Missouri. Dodd does not play up the James brothers as heroes, nor their mother as a conscienceless defender of her sons. She does demonstrate how their wartime pursuits with Quantrill's raiders (Zerelda and her toddlers spent a few nights in prison because of this) forged the connections and skills later used for train and bank robberies. Zerelda sees their deeds solely through newspapers while she fends off the Pinkerton agents (who once bombed her house), curiosity seekers, and bounty hunters. This formidable woman, who regretfully had to hospitalize her addled, aggressive husband, lived on in the old homestead until her death at eighty-six. Dodd lends depth to cowboy legends with her fiction.

Kelton, Elmer. *The Man Who Rode Midnight.* 1987. Doubleday, $16.95; Bantam, paper, $2.95.

Kelton's story tells of an aging cowboy, Wes Hendrix, who was once a rodeo star but is now the town villain because he refuses to sell his ranch and see the land flooded to make a lake for tourists. The fading town could definitely use the boost that would result from new resorts and condos being built around the proposed lake. Wes's son figures his dad should be ready to retire after nearly seven decades of hard work, so he sends Jim Ed (Wes's grandson) to talk some sense into the old man. Jim Ed shows up and seems to be nearly as recalcitrant and ornery as his grandfather. This college boy adapts very slowly (even painfully, after a few falls from a suspicious horse) to the regime of his grandfather's working ranch. There are fences to build, cows to milk, and chickens, sheep, and horses to care for. As Wes explains, "a man needs regular chores, otherwise he loses the order of life." On his second day, Jim Ed is caught up in the excitement of a neighbor's cattle roundup. As well as facing reluctant cows and a willful horse, Jim Ed meets the antagonistic Glory B., heir to the large neighboring ranch. Her taunting of the city slicker both puzzles and riles him. As their prickly romance blooms, Kelton also fills in the past loves and adventures of Wes Hendrix. Jim Ed's affection for and understanding of his grandfather also grows. Characters adapt far more easily than in real life, but the fisticuffs, romance, bad guys versus old-timers, and a neatly coiled ending provide fun reading for Western fans.

Wheeler, Richard S. *Richard Lamb.* 1987. Walker, $16.95.

Wheeler has named his Western simply *Richard Lamb* as if readers should already be acquainted with the indomitable figure whose adventures fill this novel's pages. Within a page or two, Wheeler manages to fulfill this assumption. Here is an early description: "Like Job, Richard Lamb was content to live out his old age surrounded by things he loved. . . . He was seventy-seven, having been born an hour into the new century, on January 1, 1800." He had been reared in Amherst, Massachusetts, and had studied at Harvard "until he grew bored with words and paper." He lived an adventurous life as an explorer and trapper. In 1850 "he settled at last . . . with his young Siksika wife, Aspen, and their twin five-year-old daughters. . . . he slowly erected a great, solid longhouse. . . . It was to be both a home and a trading post." In these first pages Wheeler defines a tranquil, prosperous life for this learned, capable, aging man surrounded by his family—children, grandchildren, and in-laws of the Siksika tribe. When a U.S. Army squad arrives they are readily seen as intruders, destroyers of civilization rather than the flag bearers they pompously assume themselves to be. Captain Joseph Partridge, a petty, posturing man egged on by his vainglorious brother, a New York journalist, disrupts this peaceful trading post with orders for immediate departure to a reservation. Partridge oversteps his orders, and Lamb's reasonable request for a day to pack is arrogantly dismissed. War is declared between these two strong-minded men; minor skirmishes, hostage-taking, and wily escapes take place. No one really triumphs from the brutal vengeance but at least Lamb is not defeated. Wheeler has written a spirited tale of the Old West and old age.

Short Stories

Allen, Mary C., ed. *Favorite Animal Stories in Large Print.* 1987. G. K. Hall Large Print Books, $19.95.

Allen, Mary C., ed. *Great Ghost Stories in Large Print.* 1988. G. K. Hall Large Print Books, $18.95.

Allen has chosen animal tales by such authors as Mark Twain, Rudyard Kipling, Joy Adamson, James Thurber, Gerald Durrell, and E. B. White for this large-print anthology. Nonfiction as well as fiction can be found amid these sentimental, amusing, and descriptive stories.

For the second large-print anthology Allen has selected thirteen old-fashioned ghost tales. Among the eerie and amusing stories are "The Signalman" by Charles Dickens, "Pomegranate Seed" by Edith Wharton, and "The Empty House" by Algernon Blackwood. Many are well-known spooky stories that are fun to peruse again and great for reading aloud. Because the authors are so famous, Allen offers only a perfunctory introduction to each, with few suggestions for further reading. These conventional, useful collections are a sample of the selections available from the G. K. Hall Large Print series.

Ballantyne, Sheila. *Life on Earth.* 1988. Simon & Schuster, $16.95.

In this selection of ten stories, Ballantyne explores the lives of families in some of their most sensitive moments. She wastes no time diving into the most traumatic of all as she pours out a woman's grief over the death of her parents. The impact of her emotional turmoil on her husband, family, and self is conveyed in a surrealistic conversation wherein she lists her choices of cemeteries, markers, and final resting places. A joltingly more realistic story follows. "Flaubert in Miami Beach" recounts a cross-country trip and the rainy week spent in Florida by a California family of four. They are traveling to visit grandparents whom the children have not yet met. When they arrive, the kids are ignored. The children murmur, "'Grandma and Grandpa don't like us. They're disappointed.'" Reassurances about the older people's private troubles, which they insist their grown son solve, barely placate his disillusioned children. In another story, Ballantyne realistically portrays the tedium and sadness experienced by a caring son and his wife as they search for a nursing home for his eighty-year-old mother. Her point of view is ably presented as well. Ballantyne's images of surgery, recovery, death, grief, and love are bright although based on very distressing topics. The genuine concern within her words and characters may sustain readers through incidents just like the ones she describes.

Bates, H. E. *My Uncle Silas.* 1984. Graywolf, $14.00; paper, $7.00; G. K. Hall Large Print Books, $13.50.

Originally published in 1939, Bates's fourteen wonderful stories tell of a young man's visits to his much beloved great-uncle Silas. This "rural reprobate" lived in a stone, reed-thatched cottage with an equally stony-faced housekeeper. Her starched stiffness recedes infrequently; once she seems to smile when correcting Silas's story about a group of girls who stole his clothes and those of his boyhood friends as they swam "buck naked in the mill-brook." Silas spends his days tending a garden of hearty vegetables and special fruits cultivated especially for his personal wine-making. Then, sitting with a glass of cowslip or dandelion wine, Silas regales his nephew with tall tales of his youth, when he captured the hearts of young ladies and defeated his more athletic competitors without a thought to fair play. He beat the town's strongest man by filling him with beer and pickles for weeks, until he was so bloated that the battle was easily won; he tells of eating stewed nails for a week when trapped in a cellar by the importune arrival of a jealous husband. These old-fashioned tales are highlighted by Edward Ardizzone's pen-and-ink sketches. Of these, Bates's own description serves best: "crabbed and crusty pictures . . . absolutely and perfectly in the spirit of every page they illustrate." Thus Silas's spirit, so highly entertaining, is nicely honored.

Krist, Gary. *The Garden State: Short Stories by Gary Krist.* 1988. Harcourt, $16.95.

Krist writes with loving care and disarming humor in these eight stories on family life. Hailing from New Jersey, the author sets some of his tales in the Garden State, but they could occur anywhere. Most significantly, in several of them he poses teenage characters as defenders of the elderly. In one of them, teenager Mark earns a job as eulogist after writing a sensitive piece for his Uncle Louie when no one else in the family could muster kind words. The funeral director hires him to speak for other elderly clients who have no available or willing family or friends. Mark becomes so vocal a champion of the deceased that his job is at risk and his focus in life becomes disoriented. A sudden jolt of real life is delivered to Mark as the story ends. Another young man battles to defend his grandmother against the family's diagnosis of Alzheimer's disease. Ralph obediently fetches carton after carton of unneeded milk for his grandmother rather than reveal to her, or his mother, how forgetful his grandmother has become. In general the collection is not one on aging but Krist's creation of absurd family clashes and love affairs is appealing and may be shared by teens and their grandparents.

Menaker, Daniel. *The Old Left.* 1987. Knopf, $15.95; Penguin, paper, $5.95.

The perspective in these eight sharp, revealing stories is that of a young man coping with the eccentricities and frailties of his beloved but frustrating uncle, Sol. David Leonard is a twenty-six-year-old college professor in the opening story. By the final one, twenty years later, he is an enchanted father who must juggle his energy between his two-year-old and his demanding, ailing uncle. As his stories move on in a vaguely sequential fashion, Menaker fills in the details of Leonard's family background while telling of his education, stint as a private detective, absorption in fatherhood, and attention to his curmudgeonly, irrepressible uncle. His family represents the quintessential Old Left and Sol is the most representative of them all. In order to convince his uncle to take advantage of necessary social services provided by the local Council on Aging, Leonard convincingly argues that "he would be helping the cause of Socialism if he availed himself of free government services." Sol's political fervor, often a disguise for stubbornness, adds humor to these entertaining short stories.

Sanford, Annette. *Lasting Attachments*. 1989. Southern Methodist Univ. Pr., $12.95.

Sanford has composed eleven lovely, well-crafted stories. Her title work dwells on the effect of an inherited photograph upon an enduring marriage. Over the years of their own marriage, a couple have envisioned the life of a man and woman they know only from an old family photograph. Their imaginative version reflects the sorrows and upbeat moments of their own relationship. In "Standing By" a grown daughter enthusiastically anticipates a visit to see her mother: "She is my mother, but she is a favorite friend as well." Yet in "Signs of Habitation" an elderly, ailing woman hatches a plot to announce her death prematurely to her distant offspring. She wishes to make a few "personal bequests" but would rather coerce than beg them to visit. Many of these stories feature older people whose artlessness is sympathetically, genuinely relayed. Her characters address their challenges realistically through a blend of bravery, crankiness, and pathos. Most of all, Sanford's tales reflect the difficulties and blessings of family members sharing time, knowledge, and grief.

Sennett, Dorothy, ed. *Full Measure: Modern Short Stories on Aging*. 1988. Graywolf, paper, $10.00.

Sennett has pulled together some absolutely stunning selections for this innovative collection. She has looked to masters of the short story—John Cheever, Hortense Calisher, Saul Bellow, and twenty others— to share their perceptions on aging. These authors portray the complexity of life as intensifying as people grow older. There is such a range of settings, action, and characters that stereotypes are banished. In "The Dust of Yuri Serafimovich" by James Fetter, an elderly Russian, still carrying the dust of his homeland (literally—he has a box of earth), is given shelter by the owner of a used bookstore who can turn away neither the elderly immigrant nor his ancient, unsellable tomes on the wildlife of the Ukraine in 1897. Bernard Malamud's "In Retirement" reveals an older gentleman who accidentally, then deliberately, intercepts the mail of another tenant in his apartment building to contrive a romantic encounter. In V. S. Pritchett's "Tea with Mrs. Bittell," a pleasant tea party and an exchange of confidences lead to a burglary that the old woman stops with amazing valor. These stories, rife with adventure and dignity, offer marvelous reading for everyone.

Singer, Isaac Bashevis. *Old Love.* 1979. Farrar, $10.95; Fawcett, paper, $2.50.

In the introduction preceding these ten wonderful stories, Singer explains, "The love of the old and the middle-aged is a theme that is recurring more and more in my works of fiction. . . . Literature has neglected the old and their emotions. The novelists never told us that in love, as in other matters, the young are just beginners and that the art of loving matures with age and experience." This novelist tells us about love in ways both amusing and moving. His viewpoint changes from that of a young boy eavesdropping on the clustered women in the *shtetl* to that of an older man, an author seduced wherever he travels. Scandal, portent, and human passion fill these pages from a sage, old-fashioned storyteller. His life story is told on video (see page 118).

See also *When I Am Old I Shall Wear Purple*, edited by Sandra Martz (page 105), and *Sister Age* by M. F. K. Fisher (page 5).

Organizations and Associations

The following addresses and phone numbers are for organizations and agencies mentioned throughout this guide plus others that can be a useful source of further information. Current at publication, these may change; however, updated information is available in the *Encyclopedia of Associations* (Gale, annual).

American Association of Retired Persons (AARP), 1909 K Street N.W., Washington, DC 20049. Phone: (202) 872-4700.

AARP operates AgeLine: A Database on Middle Age and Aging. For information contact: AgeLine Database Coordinator, AARP Resource Center, 1909 K Street, N.W., Washington DC 20049. Phone: (202) 728-4880.

Children of Aging Parents CAPS Office, 2761 Trenton Road, Levittown, PA 19056. Phone: (215) 945-6900.

Elder Craftsmen, 135 E. 65th Street, New York, NY 10021. Phone: (212) 861-5260.

Elderhostel, 80 Boylston Street, Suite 400, Boston, MA 02116. Phone: (617) 426-8056.

The Gray Panthers, 311 S. Juniper Street, Suite 601, Philadelphia, PA 19107. Phone: (215) 545-6555.

Jewish Association for Services for the Aged, 40 W. 68th Street, New York, NY 10023. Phone: (212) 724-3200.

Little Brothers—Friends of the Elderly, 1658 W. Belmont Avenue, Chicago, IL 60657. Phone: (312) 477-7702.

National Association of Area Agencies on Aging, 600 Maryland Avenue, S.W., Washington, DC 20024. Phone: (202) 484-7520.

National Council on Aging, 600 Maryland Avenue, S.W., Washington, DC 20024. Phone: (202) 479-1200.

National Hospice Organization, 1901 N. Moore, Suite 901, Arlington, VA 22209. Phone: (703) 243-5900.

National Indian Council on Aging, P.O. Box 2088, Albuquerque, NM 87103. Phone: (505) 766-2276.

National Interfaith Coalition on Aging, 298 S. Hull Street, P.O. Box 1924, Athens, GA 30603. Phone: (404) 353-1331.

National Senior Sports Association, 10560 Main Street, Fairfax, VA 22030. Phone: (703) 385-7540.

Older Women's League, 730 11th Street, N.W., Suite 300, Washington, DC 20001. Phone: (202) 783-6686.

Social Security Administration Office of Public Affairs, 6401 Security Boulevard, Baltimore, MD 21235 (for general information; for specifics, call the local office).

Organizations and agencies can also supply information and arrange support groups for victims of severe illnesses that often strike older persons. Below is only a sample of the sources for helpful information and support. Others can be found in the *Encyclopedia of Associations* or in books cited throughout this guide, such as *The Age Care Sourcebook* by Jean Crichton (see page 4).

Alzheimer's Disease and Related Disorders Association, 70 E. Lake Street, Chicago, IL 60601. Phone: (800) 621-0379; in Illinois: (800) 572-6037.

American Cancer Society, 1599 Clifton Road, Atlanta, GA 30329. Phone: (404) 320-3333.

American Heart Association, 7320 Greenville Avenue, Dallas, TX 75231. Phone: (214) 373-6300.

The American Parkinson Disease Association, 116 John Street, Suite 417, New York, NY 10038. Phone: (800) 223-2732.

Arthritis Foundation, 1314 Spring Street N.W., Atlanta, GA 30309. Phone: (404) 872-7100.

Emphysema Anonymous, P.O. Box 3224, Seminole, FL 33542. Phone: (813) 391-9977.

United Ostomy Association, 36 Executive Park, Suite 120, Irvine, CA 92714. Phone: (714) 660-8624.

Index

Compiled by Julie Mueller

Denise Perry Donavin is an assistant editor for Adult books, *Booklist* magazine. She received her MSLS from Wayne State University and her BA from Marquette University. Donavin is also the compiler of a bibliography, "Summer Vacations/Family Style," for *Booklist*.